The Lovers

ANNIVERSARY WALTZ

Anniversary Waltz

A new comedy by

Jerome Chodorov *and* Joseph Fields

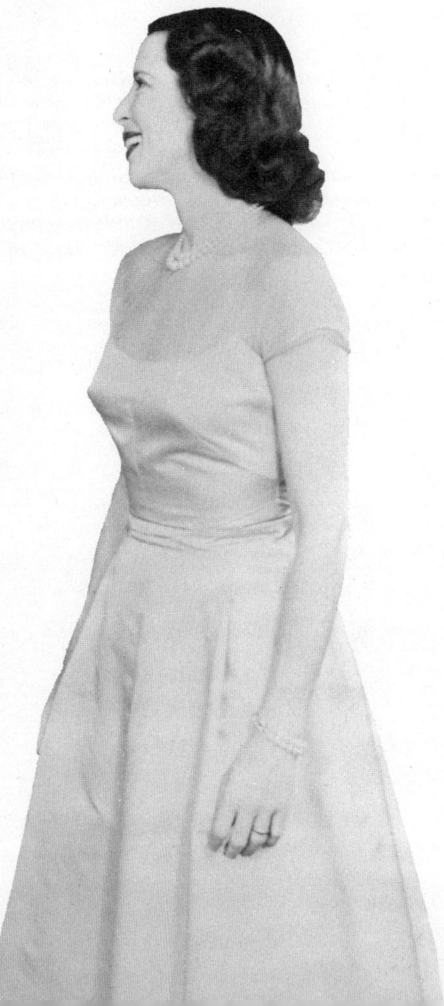

Random House
New York

Photographs by courtesy of Eileen Darby, Graphic House, Inc.

MANUFACTURED IN THE
UNITED STATES OF AMERICA

To Kitty Carlisle

Wife, Mother and our Favorite Actress

ANNIVERSARY WALTZ *was first presented by Joseph M. Hyman and Bernard Hart at the Broadhurst Theatre, New York City, on April 7, 1954, with the following cast:*

MILLIE	Pauline Myers
OKKIE WALTERS	Warren Berlinger
ALICE WALTERS	Kitty Carlisle
DEBBIE WALTERS	Mary Lee Dearring
BUD WALTERS	Macdonald Carey
CHRIS STEELMAN	Andrew Duggan
JANICE REVERE	Jean Carson
HARRY	Don Grusso
SAM	Donald Hylan
MR. GANS	Howard Smith
MRS. GANS	Phyllis Povah
HANDYMAN	Kermit Kegley

Directed by Moss Hart

Setting and lighting by Frederick Fox

Costumes by Robert Mackintosh

SCENES

The action of the play takes place in the living room of the Walters' apartment in New York City. The time is the present.

ACT ONE

Scene I: About 7 o'clock on a spring evening
Scene II: Four hours later

ACT TWO

Scene I: The following morning
Scene II: That evening

ACT THREE

Scene I: A few minutes later
Scene II: A week later

ACT ONE

ACT ONE

The action of the play takes place in the living-dining room of the Walters' apartment near the East River, in Manhattan. It is a comfortable place, with a mixture of furniture, old and new, all in good taste. There's a foyer upstage left, that leads to a door to the corridor outside. Another door off the foyer leads into the kitchen and to the right of the foyer alcove a passageway goes to the other rooms of the flat. Windows at right show a bit of the river in the distance. There's the customary sofa, easy chairs, coffee table, end tables and a rather handsome larger table upstage that serves as the dining table. There's a good radio-phonograph set against one wall, but, conspicuously, no TV set. The pictures on the wall are mostly reproductions, but there are one or two small oils of contemporary subjects by modern Americans that are plainly originals.

At curtain time, it's about six o'clock on a pleasant late spring evening. MILLIE, *the maid, comes in from the alcove, carrying a tray of hors d'oeuvre. She crosses to the coffee table in front of the sofa and puts it down. Then she checks the leather match holders on the coffee table, daybed table and small white table, as the front door slams explosively and* OKKIE WALTERS *enters.* OKKIE *is a fourteen-year-old boy, very wise, rather cynical and quite appealing. He's wearing jeans, a T shirt and sweater, sneakers and carries a baseball glove under his arm. His face is dirty and so are his clothes.* MILLIE *jumps, nervously, as the door bangs.*

OKKIE

Hi, Millie! What's new?

MILLIE

Do you have to bust down the door every time you come in? (OKKIE *reaches for a tidbit on the plate*) Keep off. These are for cocktails, and there's just enough to go round three times. (*She looks him over*) Okkie, you're a mess. They're gonna be here any minute—take a shower.

OKKIE

(*Cheerfully*)

I got nothing but bosses. You and Ma and that pork-barrel sister of mine.

(*He reaches for another hors d'oeuvre.*)

MILLIE

Not the caviar. Take one of the cheese.

(*He stuffs it into his mouth whole.*)

MRS. WALTERS

(*Off stage*)

Millie?

MILLIE

Yes, Ma'am?

MRS. WALTERS

(*Off stage*)

Did you put the wine in the frigidaire?

MILLIE

Yes, I did, Mrs. Walters.

(She motions to OKKIE *to get out of the room.)*

MRS. WALTERS

Where's Okkie? Did he come home yet?

OKKIE

Sure, Ma. Been home for days.

*(*ALICE WALTERS *is a very youthful and attractive thirty-five. She's wearing a rather splendid hostess gown and is very carefully done up.)*

ALICE

(Dismayed)

Okkie, look at you! The folks'll be here any second. I asked you to get back early. . . .

OKKIE

(Breaks in quickly)

You look stunning tonight, Mom—look like a high-school girl—what'd you do to your hair?

ALICE

Save your charm for Miss Klopf and the rest of the faculty —I'm laps ahead of you. For Pete's sake—get washed!

OKKIE

Okay, okay, don't get yourself in an uproar—I'm not comin' to this party formal, you know.

(He ducks past her, out of the room, as she looks after him with an exasperated look, then crosses to

the tray and inspects it as MILLIE *looks her over admiringly.*)

MILLIE

He's right, Mrs. W. You sure tore it tonight—just beautiful!

ALICE

Thank you, Millie—really look all right?

MILLIE

I'm tellin' you. Nobody didn't know you, would ever believe you were celebrating your fifteenth. Okkie's right—you look like a girl.

ALICE

Anyway, I fooled Grace Fletcher. . . .

MILLIE

Who?

ALICE

A friend of mine—'way back. . . . She said it would never last six months. (*She looks back at the tray*) That looks pretty good, Millie—sort of short in the caviar department, though.

MILLIE

Caviar's just for *tastin'*, Mrs. W. The cheese and deviled eggs are for *eatin'*.

ALICE

I know, but we could splurge a little tonight. After all, it's an anniversary. . . .

MILLIE

(*Shrugs*)

Okay, it's your money. Only you know what Mr. Walters's like when he sees that envelope from Gristede's every month.

(*She goes off into the kitchen as* DEBBIE WALTERS, *a cute girl of thirteen with bulging thighs and general baby fat, comes in from the front door; she wears a sweater and skirt, flat shoes and sloppy socks.*)

DEBBIE

Hi, Mom.

(*She heads automatically for the tray at coffee table and grabs something.*)

ALICE

Not the caviar, darling, please. (*She eyes her disapprovingly*) Are you dressed, dear?

DEBBIE

What do I look—bare?

ALICE

No, I mean for tonight?

DEBBIE

Sure.

ALICE

Couldn't you put on something a bit more festive? After all, it's a party—how about your brown?

DEBBIE

(*Quickly*)

I gave it away.

ALICE

You *what?* Who *to?*

DEBBIE

The Salvation Army. They need clothes for children—it's a very worthy cause.

ALICE

So's your father—even worthier, maybe. So stop giving away your clothes.

(DEBBIE *looks in the mirror.*)

DEBBIE

Oh, gosh! This crazy hair!

(*She shoves it down over her face in disgust. The door opens and* BUD WALTERS *enters, followed by* CHRIS STEELMAN *and* JANICE REVERE. BUD *is a very attractive man in his late thirties.* CHRIS *is a few years older and quite charming.* JANICE *is a highly decorative blonde, of indeterminate years. Right now they're all just a bit high.*)

BUD

(*Pointing to* ALICE *dramatically*)

There she stands, my friends—the woman thou gavest me. The light of my life and the hope of my fading years!

(CHRIS *and* BUD *put their arms around each other and harmonize as* DEBBIE *and* ALICE *stare at them.* JANICE *looks on, weaving a little, a lugubrious expression on her face.*)

CHRIS and BUD

(*Singing*)

"Believe me if all those endearing young charms,
Which I gaze on so fondly today . . ."

ALICE

Bud Walters, are you loaded?

BUD

Of course not, I'm just happy, that's all. (*They kiss.* BUD *turns to* CHRIS *and* JANICE) See! I came to worship at her shrine, and what happens? I'm accused of being plastered. (*He grabs* DEBBIE *happily*) Hi, Baby!

(*Kisses her.*)

CHRIS

We had a couple en route to celebrate, Alice. Congratulations, and I want to say in all sincerity I never thought it would last.

ALICE

Thanks, Chris, that's sweet.

CHRIS

Oh, Alice, this is Miss Revere . . . Janice, this is the celebrated Mrs. Walters we've been telling you about. Married fifteen years.

ALICE

How do you do, Miss Revere?

JANICE

How do you do? (*With some awe*) Say, is that on the level—*fifteen?*

ALICE

Uh huh.

JANICE

(*Shakes her head wonderingly*)

How about that?

CHRIS

She's dazed. Never heard tell of such goings on.

JANICE

Well, I mean—all that time—you gotta give people credit.

BUD

I don't know. Just read about a couple in Kansas married nineteen years.

JANICE

You shouldn't kid about a thing like this. It's beautiful. Makes you wanta cry.

(*She sniffles a little.*)

CHRIS

(*Wincing*)

Now don't cry all over again, Janice, for God's sake! Oh! There goes my damn back.

BUD

She just wound up her fourth husband in Las Vegas, poor kid.

JANICE

(Miserably)

I try. Every time I try. But it's never any damn good. (*To* ALICE, *pathetically*) What's the secret, honey? What do you *do?*

ALICE

Nothing. Marry a wonderful man who'll stand for you, I guess.

JANICE

(Looks at BUD*)*

He's not so wonderful. I had two just as good as that. But anyway, it never lasted. You must be a remarkable girl—just remarkable . . .

(She starts to weep.)

CHRIS

Come on, Honey, you better eat something absorbent. . . . See you tomorrow, Bud. We surround the kid here for lunch and lock her up.

BUD

Right!

CHRIS

Say good-bye to the remarkable people, Baby.

JANICE

Bye.

BUD

Bye, Janice.

JANICE

It was inspiring to meet you, Mrs. Walters. If one woman can do it maybe there's still hope for a four-time loser like me.

CHRIS

That's right, Honey, they're a lesson to all of us. (*Slaps* DEBBIE *on the behind*) Hello, Debbie!

(*They go.*)

DEBBIE

(*Angrily*)

Why do grown-ups think your backside is some kind of public property?

(*She goes off.*)

ALICE

Who is Miss Revere?

BUD

She's a character. Never saw a woman stash away the stuff like she can.

ALICE

Who is she?

BUD

Did you ever hear of Lusterlife Shampoo? That was her third husband—Max Lusterlife—and in that settlement she turned down cash and took half the factory.

ALICE

In her grief.

BUD

(*Owlishly*)

She has a lot of legal business in New York besides husbands.

ALICE

You've had a few yourself. Bud, you'd better change. Mom and Dad will be here any moment.

BUD

That's right. It's our anniversary. Do you want it now or later?

ALICE

What?

BUD

What, she says! You mean I wasn't supposed to get you anything?

ALICE

(*Righteously*)

Now Bud, I thought we talked it all over and it was just going to be flowers or something.

BUD

(*Nods*)

Or something. (*He takes a jewel box from his pocket and hands it to her reverently*) My darling—happy fifteenth anniversary, and the man says if you don't like it you can change it.

ALICE

(*Excitedly*)

What is it? (*She opens it and stares, dazzled*) Bud Walters, are you *mad?*

BUD

What's the matter? Don't you like it?

ALICE

It's—it's—we can't afford anything like this! (ALICE *takes out a pearl and diamond clip, not large but very pretty*) It's exquisite. Take it right back!

BUD

(*Shrugs*)

It's—it is an investment, you know. A hedge against inflation. Some of the smartest people have their dough in jewelry.

ALICE

You mean it?

BUD

Of course. . . . (*He grins*) Wear it like a hedge, and you won't feel guilty.

ALICE

Oh, my angel!

(*She pins it on.*)

BUD

(*Softly*)

You look beautiful, darling. . . . You look as lovely as you ever did—fifteen years never happened—it couldn't have—fifteen years . . .

(ALICE *turns to him lovingly, with a very shy, girlish air.*)

ALICE

I'm glad you could come to the dance with your cousin, Mr. Walters . . .

(*He laughs. He takes her in his arms and they start very slowly to waltz as they talk.*)

BUD

You are, Alice?

ALICE

Of course, I've heard some perfectly awful things about you.

BUD

Like what?

ALICE

They say you make a pass at every girl you meet.

BUD

That's true.

ALICE

And you're perfectly fickle.

BUD

That's perfectly true.

ALICE

(*Giggles*)

I think you're just awful to admit it.

BUD

Oh, I admit it, all right. What'd you say your last name was? Alice?

ALICE

Gans.

BUD

Gans? No kidding?

ALICE

Why, what's wrong with that?

BUD

My sweet little Alice Blue Gans . . .

(*They laugh and break off dancing.*)

ALICE

That's when I should've realized it was all a horrible mistake. Anyone who could make a pun like that . . .

BUD

Baby, I been thinking about us all day—how we used to be before we were married. Remember that joint on Eighteenth Street—the Fernando Arms? When we were still engaged?

ALICE

(*Smiles*)

Is that what we were—engaged?

BUD

(*Kissing her hungrily*)

Nobody ever had anything like that, did they?

ALICE

No . . .

BUD

Officially it may be our fifteenth anniversary, but not to me. I count from the Fernando Arms. That makes it sixteen. And that first year was the best.

ALICE

The very best, angel . . .

BUD

And what's more, I still feel the same way.

(*They kiss.*)

ALICE

Well, you shouldn't. It's not normal.

BUD

Don't you?

ALICE

Yes. But it's no way for the recording secretary of the Parent Teachers Association to feel.

BUD

The hell with the recording secretary. I want my woman back.

(*He starts to embrace her but she holds him off.*)

ALICE

Bud. The folks'll be here any second.

BUD

(*Sighs*)

The folks. If it isn't the kids, it's the folks—(MILLIE *enters*) or Millie!

ALICE

Get dressed. (*Pushes him toward alcove*) I'll put the clip back in the box and open it at the table when Mom and Pop are here.

BUD

(*Grins*)

You still trying to sell me to your parents?

ALICE

Don't be silly. You know they love you.

BUD

Oh, sure! And I adore them—don't I, Millie?

(MILLIE *giggles as he goes.*)

MILLIE

That from Mr. W.?

ALICE

Yes. Want to see it?

(*She shows it to* MILLIE *proudly.*)

MILLIE

Exquisite!

ALICE

Isn't it?

MILLIE

Say, I bet it cost a mint.

ALICE

I'm sure it did. Mr. Walters says it's a good investment, though.

MILLIE

I was hoping maybe we'd get a dishwasher.

ALICE

This is *my* anniversary, Millie, not *yours.*

MILLIE

He's a wonderful husband all right!

ALICE

Yes, he's a darling.

MILLIE

Except when he yells.

ALICE

He doesn't yell much.

MILLIE

Well, I've worked for a lot worse-tempered men than Mr. W. He's sure got a loud yell when he lets go though.

(OKKIE *comes in very jauntily, wearing a blue jacket, white pants and a pair of sport shoes. His hair is plastered down and he's got a flower in his buttonhole.*)

OKKIE

This okay?

ALICE

For the luvva—what are you made up for? Tennis, anyone?

OKKIE

You said dress up—so I dressed up.

ALICE

Don't be a fool, Okkie, and take off those pants and put on your regular suit.

OKKIE

(*To* MILLIE)

How can you please her? Here I am, straining myself to look good, and she's mad again.

ALICE

Stop talking about me in the third person. I'm your mother, remember?

OKKIE

Sure do. (*Goes to desk, gets a package*) Happy anniversary, Mom, and the man says if they don't fit, you can bring them back.

ALICE

Oh! Okkie!

OKKIE

I wish it was more but if Pop keeps me on that allowance I don't know how I can do any better.

(*He hands her a package.*)

ALICE

Thanks, angel—what's in it?

OKKIE

Open it up and see.

ALICE

(*Unwrapping it*)

I hope you didn't eat hot dogs for your lunch to pay for it, sweetheart. (*She draws out a handsome pair of bedroom slippers*) Okkie, they're lovely! How did you ever think of them?

(*She kisses him warmly.*)

OKKIE

I got so tired of seeing you come into breakfast in those broken-down things I figured you needed them. What's Pop saving all his money for, anyway?

ALICE

Please stop that business about your father and money— you get a very good allowance.

OKKIE

I do, huh?

ALICE

(*Firmly*)

Yes. And go in and change those pants.

OKKIE

(*As he goes*)

Boy, that present lasted a hot fifteen seconds. I'm a jerk again.

(ALICE *looks at the slippers happily.*)

ALICE

Isn't that darling of him, Millie? And such good taste.

MILLIE

Thanks. I bought 'em.

ALICE

Oh.

MILLIE

His money, of course.

ALICE

That's the important thing. (*The doorbell rings.* ALICE *looks around quickly*) Already? We're not set yet.

MILLIE

Practically . . .

(*She opens door, revealing two delivery men carrying a large TV set with a big red ribbon around it.*)

HARRY

Walters?

MILLIE

Yes, it sure is.

HARRY

Johnson Television. Where'll we put it?

ALICE

What? Oh . . . Who sent it?

HARRY

I don't know, lady, I guess it says on the card.

SAM

Please, lady, pick a spot.

ALICE

Oh, yes, of course.

SAM

Please, lady! This thing weighs a ton.

ALICE

Over there. (*Points to spot by fireplace*) Oh, no, no. Millie, give me a hand with that chair, will you? I guess you'd better put it over here for the time being.

HARRY

It figures!

SAM

I'm giving a personal prize to the first woman who knows where she wants it and puts it there.

(*They put down TV set.*)

HARRY

I'll be back tomorrow to install the aerial. Meanwhile, you'll probably get some reception if you just plug it in.

ALICE

(*Nervously, looking back at bedroom*)

Yes. Thank you. I mean—thanks a lot.

HARRY

(*He hands her his book and pencil*)

Just sign here.

(ALICE *starts to sign, when* BUD *comes in buttoning his shirt.*)

BUD

Alice, did you see my . . . ? (*He stops short and stares at the TV set*) What the hell is that?

ALICE

It's a present from someone—(*To men*) Good afternoon, gentlemen.

BUD

Just a minute! You know my vow, given at my poor old mother's bedside before she passed away—never, positively never, will one of those bloody monsters enter my living room. (*To delivery men*) Take it back from whence it came and credit our account. You probably have something *else* we can use—like an electric chair, or a portable gallows—something useful.

(ALICE *forces a hollow laugh.*)

ALICE

Now, Bud, dearest, don't be silly. I mean, we can't just send back a thing like this—why, we don't even know who it's from.

BUD

(*Grimly*)

Who do you *think* it's from—an unknown admirer? You know damn well who it's from—your old man was determined we were going to have a—a bloody television—set if it killed us! (*He rips the card off the set viciously, reading it aloud*) "To our darling children on the happiest day of their lives from Mom and Pop." Happiest it *used* to be! (*To men*) Get it out of here!

ALICE

Bud, please, we'll discuss it later. . . .

(OKKIE *has come into the room.*)

OKKIE

Oh, boy! Television! How did it ever get past Pop?

BUD

Go on, take it out before you louse up the rest of the family!

(*The men shrug and start forward.*)

ALICE

No! We've got to keep it at least for tonight—they'll be here any second!

BUD

Look, Alice, once you let down the bars we'll never get rid of it. I know. It's like slow poison. We'll be living with "Dragnet." . . . Let me tell the folks; I'll be tactful. . . . Go on, take it away. . . .

ALICE

You're just being stubborn and stupid, and I won't stand for it! They're my parents and it's just as much my house as it is yours—and we're going to keep it!

(BUD *looks at her for a long moment.*)

BUD

(*Roars*)

ALL RIGHT!

(*He stomps off as they all stare after him.*)

HARRY

(*Puzzled*)

What is it with him, lady?

ALICE

Good afternoon, gentlemen.

(*They go, then* HARRY *sticks his head back.*)

HARRY

What did TV ever do to him?

ALICE

Nothing. Good-bye.

(HARRY *closes door.*)

MILLIE

Yep! That yell came right on the button

ALICE

Go change your pants, Okkie.

OKKIE

You think we can keep it, Mom? The baseball season starts next week. . . .

ALICE

(*Firmly*)

Of course we'll keep it. Change your pants!

(OKKIE *grins and goes inside.* DEBBIE *comes in, wearing a pretty pink dress, lipstick and her hair done up nicely. She carries a small box with a glassine front which contains a corsage of orchids.*)

DEBBIE

Mom! Happy anniversary, Mom, and many, many of 'em. . . .

(ALICE *stares at her, bursts into a muffled sob and grabs her, holding her close in an embrace.*)

ALICE

Debbie, my baby! My dearest baby . . .

(DEBBIE *stares at her, bewildered.*)

DEBBIE

Holy Pete, Mom, it's only a corsage.

ALICE

I know. But—you look so lovely—you were so sweet to do as I asked.

(BUD *comes in from arch.*)

BUD

Alice, darling, I . . . (ALICE *turns away*) Oh, for God's sake!

(DEBBIE *turns to him, blazingly.*)

DEBBIE

What'd you do to Mom?

BUD

Don't *you* start! I'm sorry, Baby. Forgive me?

(DEBBIE *has seen the TV set for the first time and goes to it excitedly.*)

DEBBIE

Hey! Where'd *that* come from? *Mama mia!* Is it hooked up?

ALICE

Not yet, dear. Tomorrow.

(*She looks defiantly at* BUD.)

BUD

Sure. . . . Why struggle? It's like fighting the tide. I give up.

ALICE

You know it's not for me, Bud, but Mom and Dad.

BUD

I said I quit, didn't I? I gave one last bellow of pain, then rolled over.

(*They embrace.*)

ALICE

You're sweet, dearest, and I promise we won't play it when you're home.

BUD

Thanks.

DEBBIE

(*Examining set*)

Twenty-seven inches, Dad!

BUD

(*Nods*)

The big screen. . . . From now on that set takes over, but I'll always remember those glorious years before Liberace came into our living room.

(*The doorbell rings.*)

ALICE

There they are! Don't make any cracks tonight about this, will you, Bud? You know how sensitive they are.

BUD

I'll just thank them sincerely. Okay?

ALICE

Debbie, answer the door, will you, darling?

BUD

(*Staring at set moodily*)

"The Late Show." . . . "The Late *Late* Show. . . ."

(DEBBIE *opens door.* MR. *and* MRS. GANS *enter.*)

MR. GANS

Hello, Debbie honey! How's my baby doll!

(*He kisses her.*)

MRS. GANS

You look so sweet, my angel—what's this! Lipstick!

ALICE

She's allowed to, Mother—all the girls in her class do it on party nights.

MRS. GANS

Well, I hope you're not going to let her do everything the other girls do these days—not if my newspaper's telling the truth. Hello, Bud.

MR. GANS

Please, Lilly, this is no time to lecture. This is a happy occasion. Yes, ma'am. (*Kisses* ALICE) A happy occasion! (*To* BUD, *holding up champagne bottle, singing*) Pepsi Cola is the drink for you!

BUD

Thanks, Dad. But you shouldn't have done it. We've got our own stuff.

MR. GANS

Can't have too much of it, my boy. Not when you're feeling as high as I am. (*Turns to* ALICE) Look! Isn't she beautiful? My God, she's a picture.

BUD

She certainly is, Dad. How are you feeling, Mom?

MRS. GANS

Pretty good. My migraine's bothering me again, but I just gave up worrying about it.

BUD

You look fine, just fine.

MRS. GANS

Thanks. You don't. You look a bit tired.

BUD

(*Glumly*)

Well, I've been feeling pretty great up to now.

ALICE

What beautiful flowers! Dad, and after the extravagant present you sent us—really.

MR. GANS

Did it come? Well, now the place looks lived in! (BUD *glares and slams the bottle on the bar loudly*) We almost got the Chinese Chippendale cabinet but Mother finally voted for this kind.

MRS. GANS

Well, I thought as long as the Government hasn't recognized China . . .

BUD

Naturally, Mother. What else do they come in, Aztec?

MR. GANS

Well, if you'd rather have some other kind.

BUD

No, I'm very happy with this set. You should've heard me when it came, huh, Alice?

(ALICE *gives him a quick look.*)

ALICE

It's just so sweet of you both, Mother, and I can't tell you how happy you've made the kids.

MR. GANS

That's fine, Alice. . . . And you know something, Bud? You oughtn't to be so proud in the future.

BUD

Proud?

MR. GANS

I knew you were all dying for a set, but just because it cost a few dollars more than was handy (BUD *starts toward* GANS) you had to make out a whole sociological test case against television.

ALICE

(*Comes between* BUD *and* MR. GANS, *parting them quickly*) How about a drink? Won't you please make the drinks, darling?

BUD

(*Smiles*)

Sure, Baby. . . . Shall we start with martinis, or plunge right into the champagne?

MR. GANS

Champagne solo, my boy. Leave the gin to the peasants!

MRS. GANS

(*Sighs*)

You're not going to start with champagne, Arthur?

MR. GANS

Sure, Mother, this is a party.

MRS. GANS

Now, Arthur, don't be a fool and overdo it. Champagne murders you, and you know it.

MR. GANS

Will you tell your mother to stop worrying about me? A fella just gave me a wonderful recipe against hangover—infallible, they say—keep swallowing these, the more you drink, you can't get drunk. Cancels it out.

BUD

Hardly seems worth while, does it?

MR. GANS

Huh?

ALICE

Put the champagne on ice, will you, dear? (*Takes him away, whispering to him*) And thanks.

BUD

(*Whispers reassuringly*)

Stop worrying.

MR. GANS

(*Reads from vitamin bottle*)

Vitamin B Complex, to be used in supplementing a diet deficiency—as indicated by your physician.

MRS. GANS

(*Looking after* BUD *and* ALICE)

Read those directions to yourself, Arthur, I can't hear what they're saying.

MR. GANS

This is interesting, Mother . . .

MRS. GANS

What are you two whispering about over there, anyway?

ALICE

Nothing, Mother, household stuff.

MR. GANS

(*Heartily*)

Well, Debbie, so it's lipstick time in Dixie, huh? How does it make you feel—like Theda Bara, I'll bet—huh?

DEBBIE

Who?

MR. GANS

Who, she says! The greatest vamp that ever lived, *that's* who!

DEBBIE

What's a vamp?

MR. GANS

You're kidding, aren't you? (DEBBIE *shakes her head*) The language sure has changed, Mother! (*To* DEBBIE) You know—a siren—a female adventuress—breaking men's hearts and poisoning their souls.

DEBBIE

(*Casually*)

Oh, yes—a prostitute.

(*They stare at her and gasp.*)

MRS. GANS

Alice! Where did she hear that word?

ALICE

I don't know, Mother—but don't ask her what else she knows, if you want to stay happy.

MRS. GANS

I think it's just revolting! A child like that knowing such things! What kind of education and upbringing do children have these days?

DEBBIE

Is there something wrong in knowing the word or just *saying* it, Grandma?

MRS. GANS

Both! I never used such words when I was your age—or twice your age!

DEBBIE

Mrs. Wilson says that isn't true. She says there was a whole conspiratorial silence about sex.

MR. GANS

And who in Sam Hill is Mrs. Wilson?

DEBBIE

My biology teacher. She says . . .

(OKKIE *comes in, jumps over couch and goes to* MRS. GANS, *kissing her.*)

OKKIE

Hi, Grandma, whatdaya know? (*Slaps* GANS *on back*) Hi, Grandpa!

MR. GANS

Okkie, my boy!

OKKIE

You look great!

MR. GANS

Good to see you! How's the pitching arm?

OKKIE

Pretty good, Grandpa. And that mitt you sent me is swell. Thanks a lot.

MR. GANS

(*Looks at* DEBBIE)

Now here's a regular child, Alice—I'll bet he doesn't have any of those morbid, unhealthy ideas . . .

ALICE

Please, Dad. I'd rather not discuss it right now. . . .

DEBBIE

Why not, Mom? Let's bring it out into the open—that's the best way. (*Earnestly*) Okkie, do you have any thoughts about sex?

OKKIE

None of your damn business!

DEBBIE

See? Inhibited!

OKKIE

(*Clenching his fist*)

I'll inhibit you right in the kisser!

DEBBIE

A typical answer by the enraged male when he *has* no answer.

OKKIE

Why, you tubba lard . . .

(*He goes for her.*)

ALICE

Stop this—stop it at once! Okkie, apologize—Debbie, you, too.

OKKIE

Okay—I apologize.

DEBBIE

I don't see what *I* have to apologize for, but if it'll help—I'm sorry I said you were inhibited. You're obviously the outgoing, exhibitionistic type.

OKKIE

(*Raises his fist, kissing the knuckles menacingly*)
How would you like a knuckle sandwich?

(BUD *comes in with the champagne bottle wrapped in a napkin. He takes in the situation at a glance.*)

BUD

That's all—knock off!

OKKIE

Just let me do it once. . . .

BUD

I said, break it up! (MILLIE *follows* BUD *with a tray and glasses, standing next to him as he starts to pour*) Beautiful champagne, Dad.

MR. GANS

Should be good—cost enough.

(BUD *gives* DEBBIE *a glass then serves the others.*)

DEBBIE

(*Tastes hers*)
Gee—it tastes like Seven-Up!

ALICE

Not yet, dear—not till everybody's got theirs, and we have a toast.

OKKIE

(*Toasts* DEBBIE, *clicking his heels*)

Jerk!

BUD

(*Offers* MILLIE *drink*)

Here, Millie, just like in a Noel Coward play.

MILLIE

(*Laughs*)

And I hope I'm here for the sixteenth.

MR. GANS

I'll offer the first toast. I'm entitled to it, seeing as how I gave the bride away.

BUD

(*To* ALICE)

With some reluctance.

MR. GANS

Huh!

BUD

Nothing, Dad, go ahead.

MR. GANS

(*Clearing throat*)

Uuuh—let's see. . . . Here's to the loveliest couple I know . . .

MRS. GANS

I'll echo that.

MR. GANS

May they live long and happily together.

MRS. GANS

I'll echo that!

MR. GANS

Stop echoing, Lilly! And may they never know sorrow in the passing of the years.

MRS. GANS

Well, of course that's the exact same toast as last year.

MR. GANS

No, it wasn't!

ALICE

Lovely, Dad, lovely!

BUD

Thanks, I'll drink to that.

(*They all sip their wine.*)

DEBBIE

I don't see how girls can go wrong on this stuff!

BUD

May I offer the next one?

MR. GANS

It's all yours.

ALICE

(*As* BUD *takes her arm*)

Bud . . . What . . . ?

BUD

Please, a moment of sentiment is indicated. To my beautiful Alice Blue Gans—light of my life—and the woman who's put up with more, and got less in return than anyone I ever knew.

(*They clink glasses.*)

ALICE

My dearest.

(*They embrace and kiss.*)

MILLIE

(*Starts into kitchen*)

Well, I guess that means dinner.

MRS. GANS

(*As they all go to table*)

You know very well it was the same toast you gave last year.

MR. GANS

No, it wasn't.

DEBBIE

I still think it tastes like Seven-Up.

OKKIE

I like it. . . . Grandpa, sit next to me.

DEBBIE

You sit next to me, Grandma.

MR. GANS

Well, Mother, they're still using our silver!

Curtain

SCENE II

(As the curtain rises the family is sitting around after a too-big dinner. MR. GANS *is sprawled out on an easy chair, a brandy glass in his hand, humming to himself;* BUD *and* ALICE *are on the couch;* DEBBIE *is fiddling with the TV set;* OKKIE *is at the table, cracking walnuts, and* MRS. GANS *is puffing an after-dinner cigarette in another easy chair.)*

MRS. GANS

Okkie! Can't you do that a little more quietly!

MR. GANS

(Sings)

Use Ajax, the foaming cleanser! bu bu bu bu bu BUM BUM!

MRS. GANS

Arthur! for heaven's sake!

MR. GANS

Well, I like commercials, they're cute. Bu bu bu bu bu BUM BUM! Wonderful dinner, Alice. You're a lucky man, Bud—all this, and a good cook too!

BUD

I know it. Don't worry.

(MR. GANS *goes to bar.)*

MRS. GANS

Oh, now, Arthur! Not another brandy!

MR. GANS

Why not, Mother? It's good for me—I'm shocking my system tonight. . . . Besides I got these magic bullets, ain't I?

MRS. GANS

Magic, nothing! You're potted already.

MR. GANS

Who's potted? (*Holds out hand*) Look at my hand—steady as a die—look at it!

MRS. GANS

I've been looking at it for thirty-five years. . . . Put it down, Arthur.

(*The TV set lets out a loud roar and the announcer's voice comes over din.*)

ANNOUNCER

They're starting another jam! The Jersey City Wildcats take the lead! Look at that Romona Fogelson body check! What a contest this is, folks!

BUD

(*Roars*)

Debbie! Turn that damn thing off!

DEBBIE

It's the roller derby, Dad.

BUD

Roller derbies are gonna be barred—in fact, when I'm home *everything* on that untamed juke box is barred!

MR. GANS

(*Annoyed*)

Now, Bud, what kind of an attitude is that to take?

BUD

Attitude? I'll tell you what, Dad. . . . It's the attitude of a man who's head of his own house—(BUD *rises ominously, weaving a little*) king in his own castle!

ALICE

(*Pulls him down quickly*)

Sit down, King—relax. Debbie, turn that off. We're trying to talk. Besides, haven't you got homework to do?

DEBBIE

(*Coldly*)

Yes, Mother, I have. But I thought this was a party. I'm glad I put on my party dress. (*She crosses to* MR. GANS) Good night, Grandpa—I'm being banished. Children's Hour is over, it seems. (*Goes to* MRS. GANS *and kisses her*) Good night, Grandma. Sorry I couldn't stay up for the fun.

(*She strides off.*)

BUD

Why, that little . . . !

ALICE

Let her go. She's feeling adolescent again.

MR. GANS

You've hurt her, Alice—shouldn't do that to children.

(OKKIE *snorts.*)

OKKIE

Hurt her? What she needs is to have her butt kicked. You're too soft on her!

ALICE

We'll ask for your child psychology when we need it. Now, suppose you go in and do your own homework?

OKKIE

I don't have any, as it happens.

(*He giggles and hiccups.*)

BUD

How much champagne did you have?

(OKKIE *holds up five fingers.*)

ALICE

What? I didn't see you!

OKKIE

(*Leers foolishly*)

I know. Happy New Year!

BUD

You go to bed right now, wise guy.

(OKKIE *shrugs, waves at them and goes to kitchen door.*)

OKKIE

(*Stops and stares*)

Wrong door!

(*He laughs foolishly and goes off through alcove.*)

MR. GANS

(*Laughs*)

Stinkin', by God!

MRS. GANS

Very amusing. Staggering in the footsteps of his grandfather.

MR. GANS

Little champagne can't hurt him.

ALICE

You weren't always so broadminded, Pop. Remember when you thought Bud was a drunk because he took me to bars before we were married?

MR. GANS

(*Defensively*)

You were kids then. . . . *You* were a baby, anyway.

ALICE

I was nineteen.

(MILLIE *comes in from alcove, with her hat and coat on, hurries through the room, talking as she goes.*)

MILLIE

I'm all cleaned up. Can I go home now, Mrs. W.?

ALICE

Of course, Millie.

MILLIE

Thanks. . . . Good night, all.

(*She goes out.*)

BUD

She breaks like Native Dancer from the starting gate.

MR. GANS

(*A bit unsteadily, holding up his brandy glass*)

You realize nobody's offered toast—toast to happiest pair in town?

MRS. GANS

Arthur, we started that way three hours ago.

MR. GANS

We did? Well, it's three hours later. I'm offering another toast, Mother. To your *fiftieth* anniversary. I won't be here to see it. (BUD *drinks to that*) But I know it's gonna *be,* and (*Pats* BUD's *arm drunkenly, spilling* BUD's *drink on him*) that's what counts—(BUD *mops it up with his handkerchief, glaring*) My only little girl. (*Kisses her on forehead*) Thank God you're happy.

(*Drains glass, and goes to bar.*)

MRS. GANS

(*Rising*)

It's obviously time for Dad to do *his* homework, too.

ALICE

Now don't go, Mother. We thought we'd sit and play some scrabble and have some coffee later.

MRS. GANS

When your father starts crying, it's bed, magic bullets or no magic bullets.

MR. GANS

Isn't it beautiful, Mother? Isn't it wonderful the way it's all turned out? A happy home, two sweet kids, a steady good man like Bud. . . .

(*Pounds his arm again, but* BUD *has shifted his drink to his left hand just in time.*)

BUD

(*Grins*)

Thanks, Pop. I know what you mean. To tell the truth if I were you, I don't think I'd've trusted my daughter to an unemployed bum with no prospects, either.

MR. GANS

Now, Bud. That's not fair. Nobody thought you were a bum, and we all thought you had fine prospects.

BUD

Even when you chased me with that tennis racquet?

MR. GANS

Only once—when you brought her home at four in the morning.

ALICE

(*Takes his arm*)

For goodness' sake, Bud, won't you ever get over that?

BUD

Nope. He called me a no-good bum. Thought I was trying to ruin your daughter, didn't you, Dad?

MR. GANS

Nothing of the kind. I never worried about Alice for one second. . . .

BUD

No?

MR. GANS

Did I, Mother?

MRS. GANS

(*Laughs, remembering*)

Well maybe *you* didn't!

BUD

(*To* GANS)

Why?

MR. GANS

(*He puts his arm around* ALICE)

In the first place, I knew my baby too well. . . .

BUD

Oh, you *did,* huh?

MR. GANS

Yes.

BUD

(*Nods heavily, grinning at* ALICE)

Yeah?

MR. GANS

Yeah.

ALICE

Well, if you must go home.

BUD

Wait a minute. How about one for the road?

MRS. GANS

No, thanks. Dad can slide all the way, now.

MR. GANS

Just a small one, Mother. One more toast. Okay, Bud?

BUD

You bet.

MR. GANS

You give it this time, Bud.

BUD

(*Raises glass*)

To that wonderful year before we were married . . . !

ALICE

(*Hastily*)

Here's your hat, Dad. I'll call you tomorrow, Mother.

BUD

None of the responsibilities and all of the fun!

ALICE

Good-bye, Mom! Good-bye, Pop!

MRS. GANS

Well, really! You don't have to *push* us out, Alice.

BUD

(*Weaving happily*)

If music be the food of love, I'll take the overture every time!

MR. GANS

(*Stares*)

Overture? What does he mean, Lilly?

MRS. GANS

Yes, what *do* you mean? And what was that remark about the year before you were married?

ALICE

Nothing, Mother. He gets poetic whenever he gets plastered.

MRS. GANS

Stop pushing us out, Alice!

BUD

Yes! What's everybody rushing home for? Let's have another round.

MR. GANS

Okay! I'm with you, Bud!

MRS. GANS

Never mind another round. . . . (*To* BUD) I'd like a little clarification of that last remark.

BUD

If music be the food of love, Mom . . .

MRS. GANS

(Breaks in)

Yes, I heard you, but just what does it *mean?*

ALICE

(Grimly)

It doesn't mean anything.

(She glares at BUD.)

BUD

Okay, Alice, okay . . . *(He covers his mouth)* My lips are sealed.

MRS. GANS

Sealed? Sealed about *what?*

BUD

Oh, come on, Alice. It's fifteen years. What difference can it make now? They'll get a boot out of it.

ALICE

They don't need a boot right now, let them go home.

MRS. GANS

No, no! I want to know, Alice. Is it something we shouldn't know, or—or something you never told us.

BUD

Something we couldn't tell you then, Mom. But they'll get a laugh out of it, Alice.

ALICE

Bud, please!

BUD

Mom, sixteen years ago your baby was so pristine and innocent it'd make you cry.

MR. GANS

Well, what's wrong with *that?*

MRS. GANS

Keep quiet, Arthur. . . . Yes, Bud?

BUD

Mom, your baby and I had a very beautiful romance before we were married—some months before, in fact.

MR. GANS
MRS. GANS

What!

BUD

Yes! And here it is sixteen years later, and we're celebrating our fifteenth anniversary. . . . If music be the food of love, play on!

ALICE

You fool!

MRS. GANS

Are you insinuating that you seduced our daughter?

BUD

Hell, no! She seduced me. Frightening!

MR. GANS

That's a damn poor joke, Bud!

ALICE

It's the demon rum working. Why don't you go home and let him sleep it off? (*Takes his arm*) Come on, Bud, you did your bit.

BUD

(*Holding back*)

Dad, you didn't realize when you were giving the bride away, that the bride and I were way ahead of you.

MR. GANS

Now, Bud, that's a hell of a way to talk! He doesn't mean it, Mother. You made up the whole thing just to shock us, didn't you, Bud?

BUD

Nope. It's true, all right. Ask Alice.

ALICE

You idiot! (*To folks*) Let's just drop it, please.

MRS. GANS

No, Alice. I want to know! Is it true or not?

ALICE

What possible difference can it make now? We're married—we have two children—(*Glaring at* BUD) And I'm deliriously happy!

BUD

The kid's right. We're deliriously happy.

ALICE

Idiot!

MRS. GANS

Then it *is* true! When I think of the way I cried at your wedding . . .

BUD

My mother cried, too!

MRS. GANS

Your mother didn't sit on the edge of your bed, the night before you were married, and tell you everything a girl should know.

BUD

I'm a *boy*—and what I didn't know, Alice told me.

MRS. GANS

(*To* ALICE)

You lied to us. Made fools of us both, and probably enjoyed doing it, too.

BUD

Oh, she enjoyed it all right.

ALICE

Will you shut up! Don't be ridiculous, Mother.

MRS. GANS

Don't tell me not to be ridiculous. (*To* GANS) I told you sixteen years ago that they were not dancing till four o'clock in the morning.

MR. GANS

What did you want *me* to do? Hire Sherlock Holmes to follow them?

ALICE

Will you stop this nonsense?

MR. GANS

(*To* MRS. GANS)

I blame you for the whole damn thing.

MRS. GANS

Me!

MR. GANS

Yes, *you!*

MRS. GANS

Oh, I see, it's me as usual. It's *my* fault.

MR. GANS

Yes, it is your fault. You're her mother . . . !

BUD

What's everybody getting excited about? Don't get excited. It's all over now, and she's a good girl. I can prove it.

(BUD *puts his arm around* MRS. GANS *affectionately.*)

MRS. GANS

(*Flinging him off*)

Take your hands off me!

BUD

(*Hurt*)

I just told you about it for a laugh.

MR. GANS

You have a hell of a sense of humor!

BUD

(*Shakes his head*)

Look—it's history—nothing happened. I married the girl. She's got a diploma.

MRS. GANS

We're supposed to be grateful for that, I suppose. When I think of what she *could* have had. . . .

BUD

(*Starts to burn*)

Well, *I'm* what she *got,* dammit!

ALICE

Stop it! Good night, Mother—Dad—*please!*

MR. GANS

I think he ought to apologize to your mother. . . .

BUD

Apologize for what? Sixteen years ago? It's a little late for that, isn't it?

MRS. GANS

Yes, it is a little late! (*To* MR. GANS) You better swallow a handful of those magic bullets. I've got plenty to say to you. (*Turns to* ALICE) And as for you, you let me sit on the edge of your bed and make a damn fool of myself!

(*She storms out.*)

MR. GANS

(*To* BUD)

Sixteen years later you have to talk about it, and now *I* gotta go home and take the rap for it!

(*He goes.*)

BUD

(*Dazed*)

Idiots!—I mean it's idiotic—Alice, look . . . (*She turns away from him and starts emptying ash trays*) I'm sorry—I'm sorry they took it that way . . . it seemed sort of funny at the moment. (*He follows her pleadingly*) Well, what's so terrible about it? If they're screwy enough to get worked up about something that happened fifteen years ago . . . (*She slams ash tray*) Just because your mother's a neurotic woman . . . (*She glares at him*) Do you have to empty those ash trays now? (*She bangs down silent butler on end table*) Come on, honey—let's not ruin the anniversary. . . .

ALICE

Hah! Sometimes you stagger me. Let's not ruin it! What were you doing, improving the occasion?

BUD

I apologized once. I'll be damned if I'm going to apologize every five seconds.

ALICE

This is one time apologies aren't going to mean much.

BUD

That's fine with me!

(*He crosses angrily to the bar and pours a drink.*)

ALICE

Another *toast?*

BUD

(*Raising his glass*)

Yeah. To all us poor devils—*wherever* we are!

(DEBBIE *comes in, wearing a bathrobe over her night-gown.*)

ALICE

Yes, you're certainly persecuted.

BUD

And you're just as neurotic as your mother!

DEBBIE

(Pityingly)

Oh, what people do to their lives!

(They stare at her, open-mouthed.)

ALICE

(Angrily)

Debbie, were you listening?

DEBBIE

Listening? How could I help it? You know what I think?

BUD

(Dangerously)

I'll give you just ten seconds to get back in bed or you'll be hollering for a week. . . .

DEBBIE

I don't see what that attitude solves, Dad. I'm not judging you—or you, Mother . . .

BUD

(To ALICE*)*

Get her away from me, or so help me I'll . . . !

ALICE

(Icily)

Go into your room and close your door. When we want your advice we'll ask for it.

DEBBIE

And you claim to be progressive! Huh!

(She laughs derisively and goes out of room. BUD *looks at* ALICE *bitterly.)*

BUD

Another Gans! So help me God, *another* Gans! That's the terrible thing—it doesn't stop with one or two generations—each woman hands it down to her daughter, and *her* daughter, and it keeps compounding the felony!

ALICE

And the normal ones like you just sail on, picking up the pieces, is that it?

BUD

Yes! Okkie and me—we're normal! We haven't lost our sense of humor—our tolerance for the other fella's point of view—give me a kid like Okkie any day!

*(*OKKIE *slowly comes from the alcove where he's obviously been listening.)*

OKKIE

Gee, Pop, I never knew you liked me that much. . . .

BUD

Your mother and I are having an argument and we don't want to be interrupted—so get out of here!

OKKIE

I think you're *both* wrong—everybody understands about pre-marital relations today, but when your folks were kids they didn't know about things like that—

(BUD *grabs him by the scruff of his neck and the seat of his pants and rushes him through the alcove as* ALICE *stares after them with a grim smile. A moment later we hear a door slam and another moment later* BUD *reappears, breathing heavily.*)

ALICE

Put the *normal* one to bed, did you?

(BUD *glares at the TV set.*)

BUD

It's *that* damn thing! That's what started it! I knew the minute it came into the house . . .

ALICE

(*Breaks in with a scornful laugh*)

Really!

BUD

Yes, really! Ah, look, Alice—let's be sensible. I was a little high. Maybe I said a few things I shouldn't have. But I had some provocation . . . (*He turns back to her pathetically*) Now, let's start all over again. . . .

ALICE

You mean you're willing to put up with a neurotic like me for the rest of your life?

BUD

I didn't say that!

ALICE

(*From a great height*)

Didn't you? Then I suppose in my neurotic way, there are times when I fail to understand the English language, because I *thought* you said . . .

BUD

Whatever I said I didn't mean it! (*Starts to take her in his arms*) Come on, Baby. Let's go to bed and forget it.

ALICE

You go to bed, Bud. You go to bed and forget it.

BUD

Come on, darling—it's our anniversary.

ALICE

No, Bud. Our anniversary was last night. . . . (*Looks at watch*) It's exactly twelve-five. Just in time for "The Late Show."

(*She turns it on.*)

BUD

You're not going to needle *me!*

(*He goes off.* ALICE *sits in chair. Signature music of "The Late Show."*)

ANNOUNCER

Good morning, folks. We're back again with your favorite midnight program, "The Late Show." Tonight we have a special feature for you. For the first time in the Metropolitan area, we bring you "The Big Touchdown," starring Jack Oakie and Bessie Love.

(*Football song comes over.* BUD *comes back into room.*)

BUD

Are you gonna stay in here with Jack Oakie and Bessie Love, or are you coming to bed?

ALICE

I'm not a bit sleepy, thank you.

BUD

Turn that damn thing off!

ALICE

While you're up, would you mind switching off the light? I think the picture is clearer that way.

(BUD *glares at the set, then something uncontrollable comes over him and he rushes to the set, kicking it in. There's a puff of smoke, an explosion, and the sound dies down with a terrible groan.*)

ALICE

(*Gasps*)

What did you do? What did you do?

(OKKIE *and* DEBBIE *rush on.*)

BUD

(*Staring at set*)

I—didn't know I was going to kick it—honest, I didn't, Alice.

OKKIE

There goes the ball game.

ALICE

Go to bed. Go to your rooms and stay in your rooms.

BUD

(*Bewildered*)

I didn't know I was going to do it.

(*He goes to her.*)

ALICE

Leave me alone!

BUD

Alice!

ALICE

Leave me alone—and I mean *alone!*

(*She exits, slamming door as* BUD *goes to the bar and pours a big hooker.*)

Curtain falls

ACT TWO

ACT TWO

SCENE I

The following morning, almost noon.

At rise BUD *is asleep on the daybed, a pillow under his head, a blanket wrapped around him. He is in his shorts and T shirt, his pants are thrown over a chair. He turns and groans in his sleep.* MILLIE *enters from the kitchen with the vacuum cleaner, plugs it in and it starts going.* BUD *leaps up, grabbing his head.*

BUD

Millie!

(MILLIE *jumps and shuts it off.*)

MILLIE

Well, I heard you talkin', Mr. W., and I got a big day. After I clean up I got all that flat silver to do.

BUD

(*Sighs*)

Okay, Millie. Just give me five seconds' head start.

(MILLIE *goes into kitchen as* DEBBIE *comes in from corridor with aspirin and glass of water.*)

DEBBIE

Here you are, Father.

BUD

Thank you, Daughter.

(*He takes the pills and swallows the water.* DEBBIE *shakes her head.*)

DEBBIE

(*Earnestly*)

Daddy, can I have a talk with you?

BUD

No. Go out in the air.

DEBBIE

I just came *in.*

BUD

Well, go up and play with Diane.

(*Gives her glass back.*)

DEBBIE

(*Coldly*)

I just *left* Diane.

(*He groans and sinks back onto couch and pulls blanket over his head.* OKKIE *comes in wearing bathrobe and pajamas from alcove and goes to* DEBBIE.)

OKKIE

Boy, what a headache I got! I'll bet it's a hangover, huh?

DEBBIE

(*Indicates* BUD)

Sh!

OKKIE

(*Stares*)

Hey, *that's* what happened to my pillow and blanket. He pulled 'em right out from under me and I never even woke up! (*Delighted*) Boy, I musta been *plastered!*

(*The doorbell rings.*)

BUD

(*Groans*)

Oh, for God's sake!

(DEBBIE *tiptoes to door and opens it up as* MILLIE *comes out of the kitchen. A man is revealed in work clothes and carrying a large tool kit.*)

HARRY

Good morning—Walters?

DEBBIE

(*Indicates* BUD)

Sh, my father isn't well.

(*Man looks at* BUD, *and whispers hoarsely.*)

HARRY

Johnson Television. I've come to install the TV set.

(*He sees broken TV set and stops.*)

OKKIE

Oh, Jack.

HARRY

(*Awed*)

What—what happened? You drop it or something?

OKKIE

Uh huh.

MILLIE

I better get the Missus.

(*She exits in kitchen.*)

HARRY

(*Staring into set*)

I can't look.

(*He backs away.*)

DEBBIE

Can you fix it?

HARRY

What's to fix? (*He starts to go*) That's it, little girl.

(ALICE *enters arch followed by* MILLIE.)

ALICE

Yes?

HARRY

I was supposed to install this, but I guess it won't be necessary.

ALICE

We had a little accident last night—and—eh—it got . . . Well, anyway, what's the best way of handling it? Would you want to take it back and fix it or could you do it here?

HARRY

Look, lady, tell you what. Better call the store to send over a salesman. Maybe they'll allow you something on a trade-in.

ALICE

Trade-in? But it's brand new!

HARRY

Not any more. Terrible! If it happened in a saloon I could understand it.

(*He goes.*)

ALICE

Bud, did you hear what the man said?

BUD

Uh huh.

ALICE

Bud, I'm worried about the folks. We've got to do something about it.

BUD

(*Rising*)

Yes, sure. But first I think I'll have a shower and a shave, and then I'll get dressed—if I can make it. . . . Is your private suite open to the public?

ALICE

Bud, we'll have to do it today.

BUD

Okay.

ALICE

Before they see it.

BUD

Okay. Just get me a cup of black coffee—please.
(*Goes, blanket clutched around him.*)

MILLIE

I still can't believe it. He just kicked it, huh?

ALICE

Look, kids. One thing I beg of you—don't tell Grandma and Grandpa what happened. It was an accident, understand?

OKKIE

What do you think we are? Stool pigeons?

ALICE

Millie, would you mind finishing up in here, please?
(*She goes off.*)

MILLIE

Yes, Ma'am! (*To kids, eagerly*) Did you hear what went on last night? What was it all about?

OKKIE

Sorry, Millie. Family matter. You understand.
(*He goes off.*)

MILLIE

(*To* DEBBIE)

The in-laws make trouble? Grandma and Grandpa?

DEBBIE

That's the least . . .

MILLIE

Well, tell me. Don't be like that.

DEBBIE

Promise not to breathe it?

ALICE

(*Enters through kitchen door grimly*)

She promises, don't you, Millie?

MILLIE

I think the faucet in the kitchen is leaking, Mrs. W.

(*She goes into kitchen.*)

ALICE

That's not the only thing that's leaking in this house. (OKKIE *enters*) My own daughter—is there anyone you can trust?

DEBBIE

Gee, Mom, I wasn't going to tell her the whole thing—just part of it.

ALICE

Which part?

DEBBIE

Not the terrible part.

ALICE

There's nothing terrible about any of it. I hope you realize that, Debbie?

OKKIE

(Importantly)

Debbie, why don't you go up and play with Diane? I want to talk to Mom.

DEBBIE

I will not!

(She sits defiantly.)

OKKIE

Mother, would you mind stepping into my room for a few minutes? I'd like to talk to you.

ALICE

(Eyes him)

You can talk to me here, Dr. Freud.

OKKIE

Well, it's just that we've been studying about family relations in Psychology II. Mr. Phillips says the average American husband and wife reach an apex, then the curve begins to drop. That's the danger point.

ALICE

Just a moment. Your father and I will take care of our own apex and slide down the curve when we feel like it. I'm not having any talks with anyone.

(*She goes into kitchen.*)

OKKIE

It's a funny thing. They think Grandma and Grandpa are so old-fashioned, and they're so modern and progressive, but you notice how neither of them wants to discuss it with us.

DEBBIE

You know what? I think maybe I ought to bring this whole thing up at the next PTA meeting.

OKKIE

I don't know. They're funny about things like that. You better butt out.

DEBBIE

I won't say it's *them,* Okkie—I'm not that dumb—I'll say it's Grandma and Grandpa.

OKKIE

You get jerkier and jerkier.

DEBBIE

Well, something's got to be done, or we'll end up like Diane did with a stepfather.

OKKIE

That cluck!

DEBBIE

She says that's the way it started with her father. First he started breaking things around the house . . .

OKKIE

(Gasps)

You didn't tell that big mouth? Yackety yack! The whole school will know it by Monday.

DEBBIE

I trust Diane with my life.

OKKIE

Trust her! You wouldn't lend her your skate key.

BUD

(Enters arch, wearing trousers, shirt, tie—calls to kitchen) Alice, is it ready yet?

ALICE

(Off stage)

In a minute.

DEBBIE

Well, I'm going out, Okkie. You can just sit around and wait for the ax to fall, but not me.

(She goes out front door. BUD *looks after her, puzzled.)*

BUD

What is she talking about? What ax?

OKKIE

I dunno!

(Runs out. ALICE *comes from kitchen with coffee and hands it to him.)*

ALICE

Here, darling.

BUD

(Looking up at her pathetically)

Thanks.

(He sips coffee, eyeing her over the rim of the cup.)

ALICE

(Anxiously)

Bud, what's troubling you?

BUD

Nothing.

ALICE

(Softly)

There must be! . . . you'd tell me, wouldn't you?

BUD

There's nothing to tell.

ALICE

Maybe it's *my* fault—maybe I failed you in some way . . .

BUD

(*Trying to smile*)

You! You're the best thing that ever happened to me!

ALICE

Please, dearest. Let's at least be honest with each other.

BUD

Honestly, I'm not upset, and outside of a slight hangover, I'm very happy.

ALICE

(*Sadly*)

I know. I told the kids the same thing. We're *both* very happy, aren't we?

BUD

Yes! (*Looks at her anxiously*) Well, aren't we?

ALICE

Maybe that's why Debbie asked me this morning if we were getting a divorce?

BUD

(*Shocked*)

She *didn't!*

ALICE

Uh huh.

BUD

I'll talk to her. . . .

ALICE

Talk means nothing. Kids go by actions. Is it your job that's doing this to you?

BUD

I *like* my job.

ALICE

Or is it some unconscious fear . . .

BUD

Oh, please. This house is full of road-company psychoanalysts. Alice, look, you know what's wrong with me? With us? We're never alone any more. What we need is a vacation from parents and children and Millie and the whole damn business of living. Remember that spot in the pines up at Loon Lake? I think I could find it again. . . .

(*She looks at him longingly and shakes her head.*)

ALICE

Much too cold in the pines now. Besides, who'd take care of Okkie and Debbie?

BUD

(*Impatiently*)

The *police*—I don't know—Millie can take care of 'em. . . . Look, Baby, we've got to be on our own *once* in a while, without kids around. . . . We never fought down at the Fernando Arms.

ALICE

(*Smiles*)

What could we fight about?

BUD

(*Taking her arms and looking into her eyes*)

Let's go anywhere and be lovers again—like they say—happy as sin—just for two weeks—even if it's a motel in Jersey. . . . We'll go South. Florida's cheap now—out of season! (*Quickly*) Or maybe a cruise! That's even better!

ALICE

(*Longingly*)

Cruise? Bud, are you mad?

BUD

Why not? I'll finish this case I'm on next week and off we go. Chris will beef but I've got it coming to me. Picture it—the Caribbean—out on the deck while the sun dimples your kisser. Then into a blue-green pool . . . Tropical nights, soft music . . . Don't you read the ads?

ALICE

Are you serious?

BUD

Of course I'm serious.

ALICE

It sounds wonderful—only it's not practical. Married people with a family can't just take off when they want to.

BUD

Why not? Aren't we entitled to our own lives once in a while? Can't we be in love, even *with* two children?

ALICE

Yes, but not in the same way. . . .

BUD

Why? Are we too old and too tired to want each other?

(ALICE *looks at the alcove quickly.*)

ALICE

Bud, the kids!

BUD

They're way ahead of us.

ALICE

(*Looks toward kitchen*)

Millie . . .

BUD

(*Laughs*)

It won't hurt Millie! That's the Gans taint in you talking. Desire is something respectable married people don't have. Or shouldn't if they do.

ALICE

I've overcome *that* weakness, anyway—(*He kisses her hungrily*) Oh, Bud, let's never do this to each other again.

BUD

(*Softly*)

Never . . . Now how about that cruise?

ALICE

Not now, dearest. We'll have lots of time when the kids grow up.

BUD

We'll have time, but how do we know we'll still feel the same way?

ALICE

We will. I promise.

BUD

I'll settle for *one* week. (*Bell rings. He glares at it impatiently*) Never mind, Millie!

(*As* BUD *goes to door,* ALICE *closes TV set.* BUD *opens door, revealing* CHRIS.)

CHRIS

(*Cheerfully*)

Hi, son! Hello! Hello! Congratulations again. How was the party last night?

ALICE

Great.

CHRIS

What time did you break up?

BUD

Oh, pretty early.

ALICE

We were all kind of tired.

CHRIS

This is it, kid. J Day! She's waiting over at "21" for us. Even my back feels good today.

BUD

Huh? Who's waiting?

CHRIS

Janice! She's ready to sign. Just one little shove. So get your coat on—we've got a big deal.

BUD

I—I can't make it, Chris. You go. You can handle her. You're the romance department.

CHRIS

What's the matter with him? Is he sick?

ALICE

A little, I think.

CHRIS

Too much anniversary last night, huh?

BUD

That's part of it.

CHRIS

Why do you drink? You know you can't handle it.

BUD

Do you mind if I *try?*

CHRIS

(*Notices set*)

Well, so you finally got a set, huh? How the mighty have fallen! How did you do it, Alice?

ALICE

It was a present from my folks.

CHRIS

Welcome to the club, son! (*He goes to set*) Ah, the big screen, eh? Twenty-seven inches? (*Opens door*) R.C.A. or Philco? (*Stares*) Wow! (*Turns to them*) What happened? Who did it?

ALICE

We had a little accident.

(*Makes kicking motion with her foot.*)

BUD

Yeah.

(CHRIS *looks at* BUD, *awed.*)

CHRIS

Bud—you didn't—You *couldn't!*

BUD

(*Eyes him, mimicking* CHRIS)

Chris—I did—I could!

CHRIS

Well, it just isn't *like* you.

ALICE

(*Grimly*)

Last night it was.

CHRIS

Why?

BUD

Oh, look, Chris, I'm too beat up to go into it. I blew my top—and it's still throbbing.

ALICE

(*Gently*)

I'll get your coat, Bud. Your head won't throb so much at "21."

(*She goes into corridor.* CHRIS *and* BUD *look after her.*)

CHRIS

(*In an undertone*)

She's not sore at you, is she?

(CHRIS *nods to the set.*)

BUD

That's the least.

CHRIS

(*Startled*)

What *else* did you do?

BUD

Name something. Insulted Mother and Dad—threw them both out of the house—denounced Alice—tried to break into our bedroom after she locked me out . . .

CHRIS

You had a big night, son.

BUD

(*Indicates set*)

The fun only *started* with the kick-off.

(ALICE *comes back with* BUD's *coat.*)

ALICE

Here's your coat, Bud, stand up and put it on.

(*He rises unwillingly and struggles into it.*)

BUD

(*Groans*)

Oh, Alice . . . I can't make it . . . Please, honey . . .

(*Sits again.*)

CHRIS

It's okay. I'll handle it. I'll tell Janice you're still celebrating—that'll break her up! (*He pats* BUD *on the back vigorously*) So long, Bud!

BUD

(*Winces*)

Chris, please!

CHRIS

(*Laughs*)

Sunburned, huh?

(*He waves and goes out.*)

BUD

(*Growls*)

Just because he has a bad back, he goes around trying to give it to everyone *else.*

ALICE

Bud Walters, you're not *that* sick.

BUD

(*Starts to take her in his arms*)

No, darling, I'm not. But I didn't want to see anyone today—just you.

(MILLIE *opens the kitchen door and looks in with a strange smile.*)

MILLIE

Mrs. Walters, the handyman is here to fix the bedroom door.

BUD

(*Heavily*)

Well, you know where it is. Let him fix it!

(MILLIE *nods and goes back into kitchen.*)

BUD

(*Softly*)

See, darling? You shouldn't have locked me out. Not on our anniversary. Now how about that cruise?

ALICE

(*Confused*)

Bud—I don't know . . .

BUD

We could fly up to Montreal? (*She shakes her head*) Cuba —Varadero Beach—Jones Beach! Let's go *some place.*

ALICE

I told you, Bud—this summer—only a few more months to wait . . .

BUD

(*Groans*)

Months! Then how about this afternoon? Can I have *four hours* all alone with you?

ALICE

(*Helplessly*)

How? It's Saturday—the kids'll be in and out all day.

BUD

Is four hours too much to ask? We could take the bus down to Eighteenth Street like we used to . . . Jimmy's for lunch first, then the Fernando Arms . . .

ALICE

(Longingly)

Oh, it sounds wonderful. . . .

BUD

We're off!

(He takes her hand.)

ALICE

Wait a minute. I can't just walk out.

BUD

Why not?

ALICE

Where's Okkie?

BUD

In his room!

ALICE

Where's Debbie?

BUD

Analyzing the elevator boy.

ALICE

I'll have to tell Millie *something.*

BUD

Don't tell her anything. Don't look back or we're lost!

(He urges her to door again.)

ALICE

All right. (*She giggles expectantly and runs off. Her voice off stage*) And on the way downtown, let's stop in at the folks', and straighten things out . . .

BUD

(*Quickly*)

Not on the way down—on the way back—and don't worry, I'll square it. I'll be a model son-in-law. We'll take 'em out to dinner.

ALICE

(*Enters, putting on coat*)

Promise?

BUD

Absolutely! Maybe I ought to take a valise with us. The Fernando Arms may not be as broadminded as it used to be.

ALICE

(*Giggles*)

Bud, really! You're shameless!

(*He opens the hall closet, and lifts out a small overnight bag, hefting it thoughtfully.*)

BUD

This should do it. Weight's right. What's in it?

(*He opens it and takes out a pair of* OKKIE'S *ice skates, dangling them.*)

ALICE

(*Laughing*)

Okkie's racing skates . . .

(BUD *laughs and dumps them back into bag.*)

BUD

Perfect!

(MILLIE *comes in from kitchen and sees them at the door.*)

MILLIE

You going out, Mrs. W.?

BUD

(*Quickly*)

Yes. Just a few hours' parole. But don't worry, Warden—we'll be back!

(*He laughs, grabs* ALICE *with one hand, holding the bag with the other and pulls her out as* MILLIE *stares after them wonderingly.*)

Curtain falls

SCENE II

MRS. GANS *is on the terrace, pacing and smoking a cigarette. The doorbell rings.* MILLIE *enters from kitchen. She goes to front door and opens it, admitting* MR. GANS *who is carrying a large box of flowers.*

MR. GANS

(*Marches in, singing*)

"Say it with roses,
Fresh, lovely roses . . ."
(*He stops*)
Where *is* everybody?

MILLIE

They're not in, Mr. Gans. I'll put them in a vase.
(*Takes box and goes off.*)

MRS. GANS

(*Leaning in window*)

Well, well—do I hear the voice of Firestone?

MR. GANS

Now, look, Lillian. I've just brought them a dozen American Beauty Roses, and if you've come here with a chip on your shoulder, please do me a favor and go home.

MRS. GANS

As it happens, Arthur, I've been waiting here to tell them *they* were absolutely right last night, and *we* were absolutely wrong.

MR. GANS

(*Stunned*)

What!

MRS. GANS

Yes.

MR. GANS

You kept me up till five this morning, telling me how terrible your daughter was and what a dirty scoundrel she married!

MRS. GANS

(*Airily*)

I've changed my mind, Arthur. They were right. I was wrong.

MR. GANS

(*Open-mouthed*)

You were wrong, Lillian?

MRS. GANS

Yes. I think there's much too much emphasis placed on sex in America.

MR. GANS

I'm tuned in wrong. What channel are you on?

MRS. GANS

They understand these things and accept them much better on the continent.

MR. GANS

Continent? *What* continent? What the hell are you talking about?

MRS. GANS

Well, in France, for instance, Arthur, sex is an everyday thing—it's taken for granted. *Honi soit qui mal y pense.*

MR. GANS

What was that?

MRS. GANS

Evil be to him who evil thinks.

MR. GANS

(Snarls)

When did you get to France? Welcome home. Have a nice trip?

MRS. GANS

As a matter of fact I've just come from a long talk with Marcel.

MR. GANS

Marcel?

MRS. GANS

My hairdresser.

MR. GANS

How do you like that! I yell my lungs out all night long and I can't get through to you, but a hairdresser called Marcel . . . !

MRS. GANS

Now, wait a minute. Arthur, I've never told you this, but every time I'm in trouble, every time there's a crisis in our family, I always go and talk it over with Marcel. You may not know it, but you've got a lot to thank him for. That air-conditioner in the bedroom, for instance. He said you were right and *I* was wrong.

MR. GANS

Thanks, Marcel.

MRS. GANS

And when I told him about last night, he said: "Madame, *c'est charmant.*" Then he said they were so young. Who did it hurt? You? Your husband? The people next door? He made me realize, Arthur, how hopelessly provincial you and I are. *Honi soit qui mal y pense.*

MR. GANS

Honi swa, my eye! Of all the damn fool things I ever heard this takes the cake! You go off like a Roman candle last night, keep me up till five in the morning, then you run off to some stumblebum with a comb in his teeth . . .

MRS. GANS

Stumblebum! He does the Duchess of Windsor!

MR. GANS

I don't care who he does! The point is you don't listen to me!

MRS. GANS

I've been tuned in to you, as you say, for thirty-five years, and I've yet to hear anything worth listening to.

MR. GANS

(Yelling)

Well, now, hear this!

MILLIE

(Entering, with flowers in vase)

Where do you want to put 'em, Mr. Gans?

(He goes toward bar.)

MR. GANS

Any place, Millie, any place.

(The bell rings. MILLIE *goes to desk with flowers, then goes to the door.)*

MRS. GANS

Why don't you put them on the bar, Millie—where Mr. Gans will be sure to smell them?

*(*MILLIE *opens door revealing* JANICE REVERE.*)*

JANICE

Hello. Mrs. Walters in?

MILLIE

No, Ma'am. She's not.

JANICE

Oh, what a disappointment! (*She comes into the room*) Oh, hello. I'm Janice Revere—a friend of Mrs. Walters.

(MILLIE *goes off.*)

MRS. GANS

Oh, really? I'm her mother, Mrs. Gans.

(JANICE *sits on sofa.*)

JANICE

Her *mother!* Isn't that wonderful! Makes you want to cry!

MR. GANS

Why?

JANICE

Who are you?

MR. GANS

I'm her father.

JANICE

(*Sighs*)

Both living! (*They gasp*) What I mean is, married fifteen years, two beautiful children, and both parents living. Doesn't it make you want to cry?

MRS. GANS

Sometimes.

JANICE

Oh, Mr. Gans, your horn of plenty must be running over.

MR. GANS

It just did.

JANICE

(*To* MRS. GANS)

How long have you two been married?

MRS. GANS

Forever.

JANICE

I only met your daughter yesterday, and I can't get her out of my mind. You see I just shed my fourth at Las Vegas —mental cruelty. . . .

MRS. GANS

Oh, I see.

MR. GANS

That's too bad.

JANICE

I was just ready to toss in the towel and quit the marriage bit, but your daughter has given me new hope. I just had to stop by and talk to her again.

MRS. GANS

Well, I'll tell Alice that you stopped by, and it's been very nice to meet you, Miss Revere. (*Looks at* GANS) By the way, what's it like in Las Vegas?

JANICE

Well, if you're thinking of going, Honey, stay away from the crap tables or you can blow your whole alimony. You tell me, Mrs. Gans, what's the secret of staying married to one man?

MR. GANS

I'll tell you the secret, Miss Revere! Marry a simple-minded oaf who won't talk back. And when he does open his mouth, isn't worth listening to!

MRS. GANS

(*Grinds an imaginary hand organ*)

Yes, Arthur.

MR. GANS

A man is only good for one thing, Miss Revere. It's been true since the dawn of time. Send him out with his spear, let him kill a bear. Let him drag it home. Make a fur coat out of the skin, so his mate can keep her rump warm. What *else* are we good for?

JANICE

(*Bewildered*)

Huh. I don't get it.

MRS. GANS

And if they came home to a *cold rump,* Miss Revere, they'd complain about that too. I'll tell you the real secret of how to stay married. Keep the cave clean. They want the cave clean and spotless. Air-conditioned, if possible. Sharpen his spear, and stick it in his hand when he goes out in the morning to spear that bear, and when the bear chases *him,* console him when he comes home at night, and tell him what a big man he is, and then *hide* the spear so he doesn't fall over it and stab himself. But most important, Miss Revere, is to keep your own mouth shut, and listen to them talk—talk—talk. I hope this has been of some use to you, Miss Revere. Coming, Tarzan?

(*She goes out.*)

JANICE

(*Very puzzled*)

I don't get it.

MR. GANS

Don't try. You've got the right idea about marriage: get *in,* take a quick profit, and get *out!*

(GANS *goes.* MILLIE *enters.*)

JANICE

Say, tell me, what is it with Grandma and Grandpa? Have they got all their marbles?

MILLIE

Why?

JANICE

I don't understand them. I don't understand what they're talking about.

(HANDYMAN *enters, hammer in hand.*)

HANDYMAN

(*To* JANICE)

Excuse me, lady. (*To* MILLIE) I can't fix the lock on that bedroom door up here. I'll have to take the door off and fix it in the shop.

MILLIE

(*Grins*)

Okay.

HANDYMAN

Whoever wanted to get in there, sure wanted to get in awful bad.

(*He goes.* MILLIE *goes into kitchen.* OKKIE *enters with baseball glove.*)

OKKIE

(*Staring at* JANICE)

Hi!

JANICE

(*Beams*)

Oh, hello. You must be the boy.

OKKIE

I'm Okkie.

JANICE

Isn't that wonderful! One of each kind. Oh, I'd like to tie a ribbon around this whole family and take it back to Chicago with me! Good-bye, Okkie.

(*She goes.*)

MILLIE

(*Coming from kitchen*)

Hi, Okkie.

OKKIE

Millie, who was that?

MILLIE

Well, I was in the kitchen, so I didn't hear anything. But she's been married four times and she just came back from Las Vegas. (*The doorbell rings*) You expecting anybody, Okkie?

OKKIE

Nope.

(MILLIE *opens door, revealing* HARRY *and* SAM *carrying a television set exactly like the first one. There is a card attached to it.*)

MILLIE

Yeh?

HARRY

(*Looks at* SAM *significantly*)

This is the place all right. Johnson Television. Delivery and pick-up.

OKKIE

You sure that's for us?

HARRY

Positive. Walters, 12A, right? This is the place, Sam. I told you, but you wouldn't believe me! (*Opens doors to first TV set*) *Look!*

SAM

(*Sadly*)

He sure give it the full treatment.

(*They start to exchange sets.*)

HARRY

He don't fool around, either. He wants a twenty-seven-inch screen. Gives him more room!

SAM

What did he use, a hammer or an ax?

MILLIE

Just his plain foot.

HARRY

Just his plain foot! (*They laugh*) He must be some kind of a nut, huh?

OKKIE

Don't you call my father a nut!

HARRY

Okay, kid. Don't get sore. He's no nut, he just likes to kick in television sets.

SAM

I had to see it to believe it, kid.

OKKIE

He just doesn't like television, that's all.

MILLIE

He's got a quick temper. He flares up, but he flares right down again.

(*The men pick up broken set and start out with it.*)

HARRY

Well, tell him we can keep it up as long as he can. We got a warehouse full!

(*They laugh and go out.*)

MILLIE

Poor Mr. W. Even the delivery men think he's nuts.

OKKIE

No, Pop's okay. I had a long talk with Mr. Phillips, my professor in Psychology II. He says it's a typical behavior pattern of the middle-aged married man.

MILLIE

Typical, huh? Then they must be sellin' a lot of television sets. (*Looks at card eagerly*) There's a card. A' course, I ain't a member of the family, so *I* can't open it.

OKKIE

(Picks off card)

It's to Mom, and it's sealed.

MILLIE

That's only so it won't fall out. Go ahead, open it!

(He hesitates, then tears it open, taking out card.)

OKKIE

(Reads)

"Dear Alice, once again, Happy Anniversary. If Bud doesn't appreciate you, *I* do—and for God's sake, don't let him *near* this one. Love, Chris."

(They look at each other and MILLIE *giggles.)*

MILLIE

Your pop's gonna die laughin' at that.

OKKIE

(Puts it in pocket)

I better stash this and slip it to Mom on the side. How about dinner? I'm starved!

MILLIE

You can wait.

OKKIE

Hey! The Globetrotters are playin' in Detroit.

MILLIE

The Globetrotters? Try it!

(He goes down on his knees under set and starts to plug it in. The front door opens and BUD *and* ALICE

are revealed. He's carrying the bag in one hand, his arm around ALICE'S *waist, a dreamy look on both their faces. They turn in the doorway and embrace.* MILLIE *and* OKKIE *stare at them.)*

OKKIE

Mom! You're kissing him!

(*They break guiltily.*)

BUD

We do that every now and then, Okkie.

OKKIE

You mean you're not sore any more?

ALICE

(*Gently*)

No, darling, not any more.

BUD

Is that okay with you Okkie?

OKKIE

It sure is, Dad.

BUD

I'm glad, son.

MILLIE

What are we going to have for dinner? You didn't order anything, Mrs. W.

ALICE

(*Stares at* BUD)

Oh, gosh, Bud. The *folks!* We forgot!

BUD

(*Grins*)

Yeah. I wonder why?

MILLIE

Your folks were here this afternoon—they brought those flowers.

ALICE

We'd better call them right away. (*To* MILLIE) Millie, we're having dinner out tonight.

MILLIE

(*Delighted*)

Then I might as well go home!

(*She bolts into kitchen.*)

OKKIE

Hey, what are you doing with my ice skates?

(BUD *exchanges an uneasy glance with* ALICE.)

BUD

I was skating.

(*Throws bag in closet.*)

OKKIE

You *what?*

BUD

I can skate, you know, I'm pretty good.

ALICE

(*Hastily*)

Where's Debbie?

OKKIE

(*Ignores her*)

Where were you skating? There's no place to skate now. The park rink's closed.

ALICE

Isn't she home yet?

OKKIE

And so's Rockefeller Plaza.

BUD

I went indoors.

OKKIE

And so's Iceland. Where *were* you skating?

BUD

In *Brooklyn*. I know a place in Brooklyn. Who are you, Ellery Queen?

OKKIE

I can't keep up with the characters in this house.

(*He goes off.*)

BUD

(*Looking after him*)

Fresh kid.

ALICE

He's confused and I don't blame him. One minute we're fighting and the next we're laughing and scratching. We ought to tell him something.

BUD

(*Gaily*)

Tell him we're in love! (*He takes her in his arms*) "Hello, young lovers, wherever you are!"

ALICE

Only we're not young lovers. Not to the kids. We're old parties and we're not behaving normally.

BUD

Then tell 'em the truth. Tell 'em we're crazy. They think so anyway. (*He kisses her tenderly*) Oh, my dearest, I love you so much. . . .

ALICE

(*Softly*)

It didn't seem like sixteen years ago, did it, Bud?

BUD

(*Holding her*)

Yesterday . . . Only yesterday . . .

ALICE

And they say you can't go back.

BUD

We fooled them, didn't we?

ALICE

When we're alone, we're always so happy.

BUD

But those people keep shoving in between us.

ALICE

That reminds me . . . I'll talk to Mother first. Then I'll put you on.

(*She dials number.*)

BUD

All right, dear. Take the chill off her first.

ALICE

(*Into phone*)

Hello, Sarah. Is my mother in? Oh, she has . . . Can she talk? . . .

BUD

(*Glumly*)

Can she *talk?*

ALICE

Thanks. Lying down, migraine headache.

BUD

(Eagerly)

Maybe you shouldn't disturb her.

ALICE

No, better get it over with. Oh, hello, Dad. How do you feel? (*Covers phone*) Dad's got a splitting headache and terrible indigestion.

BUD

Use Ajax, the foaming cleanser.

ALICE

Bud! (*Into phone*) Thanks for the flowers, Dad. It was sweet of you. Bud wants to talk to you. (*Hands him phone*) Here, Bud. Speak to him, darling.

BUD

(Takes phone)

Hello, Dad. How are things? Are you feeling better? Uh huh . . . Uh huh.

ALICE

What's he saying?

BUD

(Covers phone)

He's giving me a routine about women. Go out with your spear—kill a bear—drag it home—make a fur coat out of the skin—so they can keep their rumps warm . . .

ALICE

Bear? *What* bear?

BUD

(*Into phone*)

You're so right, Dad. What the hell else are we good for? (*Startled—into phone*) Oh, hello, Mother! (*He winces, then to* ALICE) She must've grabbed the phone right out of his hand.

ALICE

Well, say something to her.

BUD

(*Covers phone*)

I can't, till the round's over.

ALICE

Are they fighting?

BUD

Uh huh. Oh, hello, Mother . . . How do you feel? . . . I was only humoring Dad because he isn't feeling well. . . . Now, look, Mother! You know how I feel about women. I think they're wonderful. . . . If you're going back into *that*, Mom . . .

ALICE

(*Grabs phone quickly*)

Darling! Are you feeling better? Well, I'm sure you will when you get out into the air. We want to take you to dinner. Yes, of course, he does. It was Bud's suggestion. That's very nice of you, Mother. Will you pick us up as soon as you can? We're starved. . . . Fine . . . fine . . . 'Bye.

(*She hangs up and breathes a sigh of relief.*)

BUD

(*Grimly*)

Who cuddled you when you were small?
Who'd you run to when you'd fall?
Who's the biggest pest of all?
Your mother.

ALICE

What was all that with Dad about the bear?

BUD

(*Smiles patronizingly*)

It's all right, dear. We men understand each other.

(MILLIE *enters, her hat and coat on.*)

MILLIE

Good night all!

(*She heads for door very fast.*)

ALICE

Oh, Millie. Before you go, will you just run an iron over my chiffon? I want to wear it tonight.

(MILLIE *gives her a look, and goes very slowly back into the kitchen, slamming the door behind her.*)

BUD

You caught Native Dancer just as she was roaring down the home stretch.

ALICE

We'd better get dressed. They'll be here soon. Where is Debbie, anyway? (*She calls*) Okkie, Okkie . . .

(OKKIE *comes in the room from the kitchen.*)

OKKIE

Yeah?

ALICE

Where's your sister? We're all going out to dinner with Grandma and Grandpa. It's late.

OKKIE

How do I know? Am I my sister's keeper?

BUD

Okay, wise guy. That's enough.

OKKIE

Can I watch the basketball game, Mom?

(*He opens the doors to the set. They gape in surprise.*)

ALICE

It's fixed!

BUD

How come?

OKKIE

(*Uneasily*)

No, this is a new one.

BUD

New one? Where did it come from?

OKKIE

There was a card on it.

(BUD *and* ALICE *exchange puzzled looks.*)

BUD

(*Holds out his hand*)

Let's have it.

OKKIE

(*Scared*)

It's for Mom.

(*He takes out card and hands it to* BUD *who reluctantly hands it to* ALICE. *As she reads it* BUD *looks over her shoulder. She giggles as he burns.*)

BUD

Why, that two-bit comedian!

ALICE

I think it's cute!

BUD

He's not trying to be cute! He's just trying to make a fool out of me! And what does he mean . . . ? (*He grabs card, and reads it*) "If he doesn't appreciate you, I *do*"? (*He shouts*) What kind of a crack is *that*?

ALICE

(*Looks at him*)

Bud, remember what we promised each other.

BUD

(*Yells*)

When?

ALICE

(*Hurt*)

This afternoon.

BUD

Oh . . . Oh, yeah . . .

ALICE

No more blow-ups. No more yelling. We're going to discuss things quietly. . . .

BUD

Alice, don't forget, dear. You've got to write Chris a sweet letter and thank him. . . . How'm I doing?

ALICE

That's fine.

BUD

It's the new Walters. Son, you may turn on that beautiful new TV set, that my partner sent to your mother. . . . And I'd like to watch and see how you tune in, so I can do it when you're not here.

OKKIE

You get a clearer picture without the lights on.

BUD

Well, let's have that picture as clear as possible. There you are, son.

(*He switches off the lights.*)

ALICE

Now, Bud, don't go overboard.

BUD

No, no, I'm gonna look at that thing till I like it. (OKKIE *has turned television set on, a singing commercial extolling the benefits of the "Slumberland Mattress." Another commercial, urging everyone to call up at once, repeating the telephone number ad nauseam*) What was that number again? (*Pretends to write on his cuff*) "On sale at your friendly neighborhood TV store." (*This time it's a singing commercial for a local wine.* BUD *in pantomime takes an imaginary stein of beer in the manner of a Heidelberg student, puts his foot on the daybed and pretends he's singing a drinking song from a Romberg operetta. Smashes imaginary stein against back wall. Turns to* ALICE) So that's what happened to the "Student Prince." (*The television set says "On sale at your friendly neighborhood liquor store"*) Marvelous! Keep going, Okkie!

OKKIE

It gets better than this. They're just changing over. These are the commercials.

BUD

I like them. They're fun! Alice, see what we've been missing? (*This commercial begins with a dramatic sketch between two girls about the virtues of their "Formaid Bra" which "separates and holds, lifts and molds," their torsos. It's also a singing one, of course. It ends with the question, "Are you a girl who needs the waist slimmer?"*) Are you, Alice?

(TV *announcer, "And now, back to Juvenile Jury."*)

TV

Our next case is that of a young lady from right here in New York City. Will you please take the stand, Debbie? Miss Debbie Walters!

(DEBBIE *comes on screen and takes her place in witness box. The* WALTERS FAMILY *stares in rigid shock.*)

ALICE

(*Hoarsely*)

Debbie!

(*She grips* BUD'S *arm. His eyes pop but he can't move.*)

OKKIE

Holy jumpin'—how did *she* get on?

TV

Now, Debbie, suppose you tell our jury your little problem and perhaps they can solve it for you.

(BUD *gurgles wordlessly.*)

OKKIE

God! She's *twice* as fat on television!

ALICE

Sh!

DEBBIE

Well, Mr. Duffy, I would like to know what the jury thinks of my problem. You see, I have the nicest mother and father you can imagine.

ALICE

(*Hoarsely, to* BUD)

Bud, call up the station—make them take her off—stop her!

(*Like a mechanical man,* BUD *goes to the phone and starts to dial, his eyes glued to the set.*)

DEBBIE

But recently they had a very serious quarrel . . .

BUD

What! Why that little . . . !

ALICE

Quiet!

DEBBIE

And they seem to resent me if I try to bring them together. Now I'm very concerned because I feel that if things drift on this way any longer there may be a serious breach . . .

(BUD *utters a strangled moan as he stands there, frustrated, clenching his fists and glaring.*)

ALICE

Oh, my God, Bud . . . !

OKKIE

(*Sadly*)

Oh, you fat little jerk.

BUD

What station is that?

OKKIE

N.B.C.

BUD

Operator—what's the number of N.B.C.? This is an emergency!

DEBBIE

(*Blithely*)

So what *I* would like to know is, what action would the jury advise me to take?

THE SMALLEST JUROR

(*A six-year-old with a high piping voice*)

Well, Debbie, everybody's parents have little arguments. I know mine do, but they always kiss and make up.

GIRL JUROR

Perhaps it's more serious than you think, Patricia, but I don't believe we can help you, Debbie, unless we know more about it.

DEBBIE

(*Hesitates*)

Well, it's a sort of a—a family matter . . .

ALICE

Oh-h-h—

BUD

(*Desperately*)

Debbie—I'm *warning* you—I'm *telling* you . . . !

ALICE

Bud—get out of the way. . . .

DEBBIE

But I can tell you this—it all came about as a result of my grandparents finding out that my father and mother had pre-marital relations. . . .

(ALICE *groans and falls back in chair. The picture goes blank.* BUD *is kneeling, making soundless words —dialing. A discreet voice comes through on TV set.*)

VOICE

Ladies and gentlemen—we're having a little mechanical difficulty but we'll be back on the air in a moment. . . . Please stand by . . .

(*Organ music swells.* BUD *stares at* ALICE *with a stunned look. He throws phone in the air and starts toward the set—*OKKIE *stands on daybed and tries to stop him.*)

OKKIE

Pop! No!

BUD

(*Shakes him off violently*)

Get away from me!

(*He lunges forward and sends a terrible kick through the glass.*)

Quick Curtain

ACT THREE

ACT THREE

SCENE I

A few minutes later. MILLIE, *still wearing her hat, is sweeping up the pieces in front of the set with a pan and brush.* ALICE *is seated on the sofa, a very sober look on her face, staring into space.* BUD *is at the phone—at the desk—raging.* OKKIE *has his head halfway into the set, examining it thoughtfully.*

BUD

(*Into phone*)

Look, what the hell kind of an organization *is* this? You connect me with that studio and be damn quick about it! You got a lawsuit on your hands right now. Don't make it any worse!

ALICE

(*Painfully*)

Oh, Bud, *please!* What's the good of it? The damage is done.

BUD

(*Furiously*)

They won't get away with this! What do they mean, letting a little child go on the air without her parents' permission? How *dare* they!

OKKIE

Pop, I think they can fix this one. You just broke the picture tube.

BUD

(*Snarls*)

Get out of here! (OKKIE *hurries out, frightened.* MILLIE *almost drops the tray.* BUD *turns back to phone*) Now, you listen to me—I want to speak to that studio and I want to speak to my daughter or else . . . (*Yells*) Come *back* here! (*He jiggles hook violently*) Operator! Operator!

(ALICE *rises, has crossed to him and takes phone firmly.*)

ALICE

Bud, just forget it. . . . (*To* MILLIE) Millie, you'd better vacuum that and get all the little pieces up.

MILLIE

Yes, Ma'am!

(*Nods and goes into kitchen.*)

ALICE

I guess they'll have to invent some new material. Instead of glass.

BUD

Wait till I get my hands on that little monster!

ALICE

(*Sadly*)

Oh, darling, don't talk like that. Can't you see we have a terrible problem on our hands?

BUD

(*Savagely*)

We sure have! But I'll handle it, don't worry! I'll straighten her out!

ALICE

Don't you realize how deeply disturbed and confused the child must be to do a thing like that?

BUD

(*Wildly*)

She's disturbed! What about *me?* I've got to go to the office tomorrow and *face* everybody!

ALICE

Your office is not as important as your child's emotional condition.

BUD

Oh, please! Don't give me any of that PTA crap!

ALICE

(*Nobly*)

It's our fault, you know.

BUD

Our fault!

ALICE

We failed her in some way.

BUD

Yes, and I'll tell you how! We didn't give her a good clobber from the time she could walk. We sent her to that damn progressive school instead.

ALICE

Don't be ridiculous. The school has nothing to do with it.

BUD

It's got everything to do with it. No discipline, no schedule —no *school* half the time! Starts in October and ends in May. And two weeks off for Hallowe'en!

ALICE

If you're going to talk that way I won't even discuss it with you.

BUD

I've been fighting for years to send them to public school!

ALICE

They're overcrowded. There are no *seats* in the public schools.

BUD

Then let 'em sit on the floor where the teacher can hit 'em over the heads easier!

ALICE

Don't you care what they grow up to be?

BUD

They're growing up to be barbarians! *Do* anything you like, *say* anything you like, *express* yourself! It doesn't matter what damage you do, just so your personality isn't warped.

ALICE

That's a totally false picture of progressive education.

BUD

That's the picture *I* get, right here in this house!

ALICE

I suppose you'd like a pair of mechanical dolls, that you wind up and that do anything they're told to do?

BUD

I'd like a little respect for their parents—a sense of family pride . . .

ALICE

Then give them something to be proud of. And try to set them an example.

BUD

There's nothing wrong with the example I'm setting around here.

ALICE

Hah!

BUD

I know I respected my mother and father and if I didn't, my old man gave me a clout on the jaw, and I grew up, and I went to public school.

ALICE

Yes, and look!

(*She indicates the broken TV set.*)

BUD

I'm expressing myself. That's what they teach them in that progressive school, isn't it? Hah!

ALICE

The new Walters. No more shouting. Let me know when you want to go skating again, sometime.

(*She goes out.*)

BUD

(MILLIE *enters with vacuum cleaner, plugs it in*)

Millie, tell me something.

MILLIE

Yessir?

BUD

You've worked in a lot of homes where there were children, haven't you?

MILLIE

Yes, Mr. W.

BUD

Were they anything like this?

MILLIE

They all run about the same. They average up.

BUD

They do, huh? And the fathers—am I any worse than the average run?

MILLIE

No, you're a good man, Mr. W. I seen a lot worse. Maybe you yell a little louder, but nobody pays any attention to it.

BUD

Thanks, Millie. Maybe I just don't know how to fit into family life.

MILLIE

Nobody does. You just go from one thing to another. You just gotta play it by ear.

BUD

I tried. My God, how I've tried. I want to be a good husband and a good father. I love my family. They're all I've got to live for.

MILLIE

I know, Mr. W.

BUD

But my God, Millie. Before you're married, everything seems so simple. You're in love and that's it. You take your girl dancing on the Starlight Roof, you don't know it, but looking over that lovely girl's shoulder is the Sunshine Diaper Service. And right through the strains of Guy Lombardo, though you don't hear it, Millie, comes the roar of the vacuum cleaner. And instead of I love you, pretty soon you're looking into your loved one's eyes and saying, "The baby didn't throw up again, darling?" I tell you, Millie, by the time you get that wonderful girl you took to the Starlight Roof away from the children, your father-in-law, your mother-in-law, the PTA, the A&P, Dr. Spock and Dr. Gesell, and should they go to the same camp this summer, by the time you close the door to the bedroom at night, you're just too exhausted to give a damn. No, Millie. Love is one thing, and marriage and children are another. And never the twain shall meet. They're ships that pass in the night, Millie, one ship is you and your loved one, sending out an S.O.S. and the other ship is full of children—firing on the lifeboats.

MILLIE

Mr. W. you ought to write all that down sometimes. You could sell it to the *Readers Digest.*

(MILLIE *goes off.*)

BUD

I don't know! (*Looks after her*) I don't know—

(*He sits on couch, puzzled, then notices* OKKIE'S *baseball mitt. He picks it up and smiles. Doorbell rings.* ALICE *enters and goes to door.*)

ALICE

Maybe that's Debbie now!

(ALICE *opens door revealing* JANICE *and* CHRIS, *they are both a little high.*)

JANICE

Hi everyone! Can we come in?

CHRIS

Hello, kids.

JANICE

(*Sentimentally*)

Mrs. Walters—Alice—Is it okay if I call you Alice?

ALICE

Oh, certainly, Janice.

JANICE

We'll probably be seeing a lot of each other from now on.

CHRIS

Forgive us, will you, but we had to stop and seal the deal with a little drink.

BUD

Oh, sure. A little drink—coming right up . . . What have you been drinking?

JANICE

Scotch and soda, with a piece of lemon peel, and a dash of Pernod, but if you haven't got the Pernod, just the lemon peel, I'm not fussy. (*Emotionally*) And I just *had* to come back, and see if you folks were *real.* Or have I just dreamed it?

ALICE

(*Soberly*)

Oh, we're *real,* all right.

JANICE

You don't know what a beautiful thing it is—how lucky you are—you just don't *know!*

ALICE

(*Forces a smile*)

Oh, yes I *do,* Janice.

CHRIS

Say, Bud. This is a big occasion. Why don't you and Alice come out to dinner with us?

BUD

Well, thanks, Chris, but the fact of the matter is, I'm still pretty rocky.

ALICE

We *had* dinner already.

BUD

Yes!

CHRIS

Oh? Too bad.

ALICE

Millie just cleared the table.

(OKKIE *enters, dressed in his best blue suit.*)

CHRIS

Sorry you don't feel right, Bud.

BUD

I'll live.

OKKIE

Hi!

JANICE

Hello, Okkie! Hello, dreamboat! Isn't he a living *doll,* that kid? (*Turns to* ALICE) In a few years, he's going to be a killer! Say, where's that Debbie-doll?

BUD

"Debbie-doll" should be here any minute. We're waiting for her.

JANICE

How old is she now?

ALICE

Thirteen.

JANICE

Thirteen! (*Turns to* CHRIS) Chris, do you realize that I could have had one just like her with my first husband?

BUD

You can have Debbie.

JANICE

Gee, Okkie. You're all dressed up. Going somewhere?

OKKIE

Mom and Pop are taking us all out to dinner. Hey, Mom, when are we gonna eat? I'm *starved.*

(*There is an awkward silence.*)

BUD

Well, here they are, folks, drink up!

(*Gives drinks to* CHRIS *and* JANICE. MILLIE *enters from kitchen with a freshly pressed dress on a hanger.*)

MILLIE

Here's your dress, Mrs. W. All ready to slip on.

ALICE

Hang it up in the closet.

MILLIE

Night all! Have a nice dinner!

(*She hangs dress in closet and goes.*)

JANICE

Did you folks say you had dinner, or you didn't have dinner?

CHRIS

Yes! I'm a little mixed up about that myself. Oh, by the way . . . I sent up a little present this afternoon. (*Laughs as he sees broken set*) I guess it didn't get here yet.

BUD

Yes, as a matter of fact, it did. Alice was just going to sit down and write you a thank-you note. . . . Thanks.

CHRIS

(*Looking at* ALICE, *bewilderedly*)

Alice, what's he *talking* about?

ALICE

(*Glaring at* BUD)

Nothing. He's just being funny. (*To* OKKIE, *anxiously*) Okkie, will you go to your room, please?

OKKIE

I'm hungry.

ALICE

(Snaps)

I know, but first go to your room!

OKKIE

(Shaking his head)

The Iron Curtain falls.

(He goes off.)

JANICE

Dreamboat!

ALICE

(Trying to smile)

Can I freshen your drink, Janice?

JANICE

No, honey, this is fine.

ALICE

Wouldn't you like to freshen up before you go out to dinner?

JANICE

Why, do I need it?

ALICE

No, you look lovely—only . . . *(Takes her arm and leads her off)* That smudge under your eye. It's not mascara, is it?

(CHRIS *stares at the set wonderingly.*)

CHRIS

This is the set the *Ganses* sent, isn't it?

BUD

No, Chris. This is yours.

CHRIS

(*Unbelievingly*)

Don't tell me you did it *again*?

BUD

Uh huh.

CHRIS

You must be out of your mind! What *are* you, a *lunatic*?

BUD

(*Restraining himself with difficulty*)

Look, Chris—you don't know what I *saw* on that thing!

CHRIS

I don't care *what* you saw! No program is *that* lousy! (*He grabs his back in pain*) Why do I get excited? There goes my back again!

(ALICE *comes back into the room anxiously.*)

ALICE

Boys, lower your voices—what will she think?

CHRIS

(*Angrily*)

I know what *I* think! I got a crazy partner!

BUD

I wouldn't have seen it, if you hadn't sent me that damned set!

ALICE

Don't be a fool, Bud! It was on a million other sets!

BUD

(*Snaps*)

Twenty million! (*To* CHRIS) Anyway, who asked you to send us one?

CHRIS

I didn't send it to *you*—I sent it to Alice!

BUD

And that's another thing. Stop sending presents to my wife.

ALICE

Bud, *please!*

CHRIS

And what does that remark mean?

BUD

I know how you operate. I've been watching it for years. You've been circling around this house like a vulture.

ALICE

Bud, that's a terrible thing to say! Apologize!

BUD

Apologize? I'm sick of him, and I'm sick of tiptoeing around that lousy back of his!

CHRIS

(*To* ALICE)

My back—my lousy back—did you hear what he said about my back? Okay! If that's the way you feel about it. I hadn't realized my back had annoyed you all these years.

BUD

Well, it has. It's annoyed the hell out of me. (*Mimicks* CHRIS) Oh, my back, my poor back, can't stand up, can't sit down, oh my back . . .!

CHRIS

(*Grimly*)

So my lousy back annoys you?

BUD

Yes!

CHRIS

Okay, you buy me out, or I'll buy you out.

ALICE

Chris, please.

CHRIS

I'm sorry, Alice.

JANICE

(*Enters*)

I see you didn't get your bedroom door back yet, Alice.

ALICE

What's that?

JANICE

(*Looks at* BUD)

That's so sweet. Breaking down the door after fifteen years. You can freshen this up now if you want to, honey.

CHRIS

No, Janice, let's get moving. My back's killing me. (*Turns to* BUD) Sorry!

JANICE

Oh, you poor boy, come on, Janice will look after you.

ALICE

I'm awfully glad you dropped in, Janice.

CHRIS

Good-bye, and thanks, Alice. (*Turns to* BUD) I'll see you at the office Monday. We can draw up the papers and settle the whole thing.

(*He goes, holding his back.*)

JANICE

(*To* ALICE)

Let's have lunch together, Honey. Maybe some of your magic will rub off on me. (*To* BUD) Bye, Strong Boy!

(*She goes.*)

ALICE

Nice going, Bud. What are your plans for the rest of the evening?

BUD

He started it! And let him keep away from my home!

ALICE

(*Nods judiciously*)

I think he will. I think *everybody* will.

BUD

(*Sulkily*)

What am I supposed to do? Let him come in here and throw his weight around?

ALICE

(*Sighs*)

Oh, Bud. You don't even realize what you did just now?

BUD

(*Uneasily*)

I warned him, didn't I? He pushed me too far.

ALICE

(*Grimly*)

Not as far as *I'd* like to push you!

BUD

He called me a lunatic, didn't he?

ALICE

(*Looking at set*)

And without the slightest provocation.

BUD

Oh, yes! You don't know him as well as I do. He's circling *around* you, I tell you!

ALICE

Oh, you idiot! *One* of us has to keep his sanity around here. Now, listen to me—Monday morning, bright and early, you're going to the office and apologize to him!

BUD

I'll bring a big red apple, and an osteopath!

ALICE

I'm serious. I'm not going to let you throw away twelve years of hard work, and see your business ruined.

BUD

You don't actually believe that we could ever work together again? Do you?

ALICE

Of course you can. Why not?

BUD

What's the use? Women just don't understand the idea of principle, or honor, or self-respect. . . . He's right! By God, he's *right.*

ALICE

Who's right?

BUD

Your idiot father! Go out with your spear, kill a bear, drag it home, make a fur coat out of the skin so they can keep their rumps warm. (ALICE *laughs*) What the hell's so funny?

ALICE

Don't mind me, dear. I think I'm going crazy.

(*The doorbell rings.* ALICE *opens door revealing* MR. *and* MRS. GANS.)

MR. GANS

(*Sings*)

Halo, everybody, Halo—Halo is the shampoo that glorifies your hair! Hi, son! How about going to the Latin Quarter? I hear they've got a great show!

MRS. GANS

The kids will love it! It's so instructive!

MR. GANS

Well, it's lively and gay, and that's our mood!

ALICE

Dad, don't you think we could go to some quiet little family place?

(MR. GANS *grabs her and whirls her around in a dance.*)

MR. GANS

No! Let's have some fun for a change! I want to hear music. I want to dance. (*Sings*) Every little movement has a meaning all its own . . . ! (*His eyes fall on something on the TV set, and he stops short*) There's a scratch on it already. Careless!

(*He wets his finger and runs it over the scratch.*)

ALICE

(*Very worriedly*)

Probably did it moving it up here.

MR. GANS

Then they're responsible! I won't pay the bill until they send a man to touch it up.

ALICE

Oh, that's all right. Millie can do it.

MR. GANS

How's the reception?

(BUD *edges down to set.*)

ALICE

(Quickly)

Fine—fine!

MR. GANS

(Glances at his watch)

Say, Perry Como must be on! "Sound off for Chesterfield!" (*He reaches for the doors of the set.* BUD *tries to stop him, but it's too late. He throws them open, starts to turn the dial on, then stops and stares. In a strangled voice*) What—what *happened* to it?

ALICE

(A moan)

Oh, no—!

MR. GANS

(Hoarsely)

Who—who did it?

ALICE

Look, Pop, I can't go into it, now. I just haven't got the strength.

MRS. GANS

You certainly owe us some explanation. . . .

ALICE

It was an accident. We feel sick about it.

MRS. GANS

Accident . . . Accident, my foot! *He* did it, didn't he?

(ALICE *just looks at them, too weary to fight back.* MR. GANS *is stunned.*)

MR. GANS

You! I want to talk to you!

BUD

(*Pleasantly*)

Yes, Dad?

MR. GANS

What goes on here? What did you do to that set I gave you?

BUD

Take it easy, Pop. That isn't even *your* set.

MR. GANS

What the hell are you *talking* about?

BUD

Your set was eliminated in the semi-finals.

MR. GANS

He's mad!

BUD

That one was a present from my ex-partner.

MRS. GANS

(*Backs away from him, frightened*)

I always knew he had a temper but he never did anything like this before.

BUD

(*Simply*)

I never had television before.

MR. GANS

Alice, I'm not going to let you and the children stay in the same house with this man!

ALICE

(*Angrily*)

Pop, will you please keep out of this!

MRS. GANS

(*Crisply*)

She's right, Arthur. It's all your fault anyway.

MR. GANS

(*Whirls on her*)

My fault?

MRS. GANS

You know what kind of a man your son-in-law is. You never should have given him a television set in the first place!

BUD

(*Dangerously cool*)

I hate to take sides, but Mother's right, Dad.

MRS. GANS

(*Turns to* BUD)

There are some people you *can't* do anything for. And the more you do for them, the more they resent it. . . .

MR. GANS

(*Snarls at her*)

Yes, Mrs. Edgar Guest! I've heard your philosophy for years! Now just stay out of this! (*To* ALICE) He needs medical treatment, and if you don't take any action *I* will!

BUD

(*Taps him on the shoulder*)

Just what kind of action are you looking for, Mr. Gans?

ALICE

Bud!

BUD

(*Menacingly*)

Now never mind Alice and the kids. Just take your wife and get *out* of here!

ALICE

How dare you talk to my father that way?

(*The door opens and* DEBBIE *comes in, waving a bond excitedly.*)

DEBBIE

Mom! Pop! I got a hundred-dollar government bond for going on the program! Did you watch me on TV, Grandma? You shoulda seen me, Grandpa! I stopped the show! It's really only seventy-five dollars but in ten years it'll be worth a *hundred!*

BUD

(*Removing belt grimly*)

What makes you think you're gonna live to collect? Debbie, come here, come here to your friendly neighborhood father.

ALICE

Don't you dare *touch* this child!

BUD

Debbie!

MRS. GANS

If you lay a hand on that little girl . . .

MR. GANS

(*Menacingly*)

Don't worry. He won't!

ALICE

(*Embraces* DEBBIE)

My poor little baby. I understand, darling.

DEBBIE

(*Bewildered*)

Gee, Mom, what's goin' on?

ALICE

You're confused and unhappy, dearest. . . .

BUD

Are you going to keep on with that double-talk or are you going to let *me* handle it!

ALICE

Bud Walters, I'm warning you! If you don't leave her alone we're getting out of this house!

BUD

Oh, so that's it, huh? I've got nothing to say about my own children in my own house. All right, from now on they're your children and it's your house and I'm getting out! They fired on the lifeboats once too often!

(*He goes out.*)

Curtain

Scene II

Saturday, a week later.

ALICE, DEBBIE *and* OKKIE *are seated at the table finishing their breakfast.* ALICE *is very morose, toying with her food.* OKKIE *and* DEBBIE *watch her sadly, exchanging significant looks as* ALICE *sighs to herself.* MILLIE *comes in with a platter. She looks very depressed, too.*

MILLIE

Any more French toast?

ALICE

No, thanks, Millie.

MILLIE

Debbie?

DEBBIE

It'd stick in my throat.

(MILLIE *puts platter on table and goes into kitchen.*)

ALICE

Now darling, you've got to eat something.

OKKIE

She could live on her fat for a month.

DEBBIE

You shut up. You have no feeling. What do *you* care if your father's disappeared, swallowed up into oblivion?

ALICE

Debbie! Don't talk like that! Your father's gone out of town for a few days.

DEBBIE

Oh, please, Mother, you don't have to put on a brave front for us. *We* know.

OKKIE

You haven't heard from Pop at all, have you, Mom? (*She shakes her head, her eyes filling*) You don't even know where he is, do you? (*She shakes her head again*) Mom, you and Pop aren't going to get a divorce, are you?

ALICE

(*Unhappily*)

I—I don't know, Okkie.

DEBBIE

If you do get a divorce, who's going to get *us*?

ALICE

Nobody's going to *get* anybody. If your father and I—if it *should* happen—naturally, you'll be in my custody.

DEBBIE

I'll tell the judge that I love you both just as much—and I'll split you up even—six months apiece.

ALICE

Yes, I can see you now—Bette Davis in the witness box.

OKKIE

Will Pop have to pay alimony?

ALICE

(*Miserably*)

Please, Okkie—I don't know—I suppose so.

OKKIE

How is he gonna do it? He's just breakin' even *now*.

ALICE

I'd rather not discuss it.

OKKIE

Poor Pop.

ALICE

What do you mean, poor Pop?

OKKIE

Well, I was just thinking—he's probably alone and miserable some place.

ALICE

I'm pretty miserable too.

DEBBIE

You got us.

ALICE

(*Flatly*)

I know. (*She starts away*) Well, if he is all alone the least he could do is pick up a phone and call.

OKKIE

You know Pop. He's proud.

ALICE

So am I.

OKKIE

Well, *somebody's* gotta make the first move in a situation like this.

ALICE

Why does it have to be me? *I* didn't kick the sets—*I* didn't walk out . . . ! Look, darlings, when you grow up you'll understand. . . .

(*She goes out.*)

OKKIE

That's what they always say. (*Pityingly*) Poor Mom . . .

(DEBBIE *nods sadly.*)

DEBBIE

Yeah. I wonder why he doesn't come home, Okkie.

OKKIE

I don't know. Even if he's sore at Mom, you'd think maybe he'd miss *us.*

DEBBIE

Maybe he's *never* coming back.

OKKIE

He's *gotta* come back . . . ! (*Uneasily*) Doesn't he?

DEBBIE

I guess so. He's our father. He's supposed to support us till we get married or somethin'. (*Doorbell rings.* DEBBIE *looks at* OKKIE *hopefully and runs to door. She opens it up, revealing* CHRIS) Oh—it's *you.*

(CHRIS *comes in, hobbling painfully.*)

CHRIS

Hi, Debbie. Your mother in?

DEBBIE

Uh huh.

CHRIS

Hi, Okkie.

OKKIE

Hi.

CHRIS

Didn't hear anything from Dad, did you?

OKKIE

Nope. Did you?

CHRIS

No, I haven't. Will you tell your mother I'm here, Debbie?

(*The phone rings.*)

OKKIE

(*Grabs phone*)

Hello? Yes, she's here. Who's calling, please? (MILLIE *comes in to clear dishes at dining table.* OKKIE *calls off*) Mom! Phone!

(ALICE *hurries in eagerly.*)

ALICE

Who is it, Okkie?

OKKIE

No, Mom. It's only N.B.C.

ALICE

(*Takes phone*)

What do *they* want? Hello, Chris . . .

CHRIS

Hi, Alice!

ALICE

(Into phone)

Yes? This is Mrs. Walters . . . Yes, Debbie's mother . . . (ALICE's *expression hardens*) What? Absolutely *not,* Mr. Todman! No, there's no point in coming to see me. Debbie has been on her last TV program while she's still a minor and under my control! Good-bye!

(She hangs up angrily.)

CHRIS

What was *that?*

DEBBIE

I'll bet they wanted me to go on the panel, didn't they?

ALICE

Just forget it, Miss Television—just forget it!

DEBBIE

Gee, but a bond every week—I could buy my own clothes and help *you* out, too.

ALICE

Thanks. When I need your help I'll let you know. You've caused enough trouble already.

DEBBIE

I'm getting pretty sick of being a minor.

(She goes out.)

OKKIE

Look at her on a panel? There must be an awful lot of morons in this country.

(*He goes into kitchen.*)

ALICE

Chris, have you heard anything? (*She breaks off as she realizes* MILLIE *is listening*) That'll be all, Millie.

MILLIE

All what?

ALICE

Finish the ironing.

MILLIE

I did finish.

ALICE

Then do something else—in the kitchen.

MILLIE

Okay.

(*She goes off in kitchen.*)

ALICE

If Bud thinks I'm going to wait around until he decides to call me he's mistaken!

CHRIS

(*Soothingly*)

Don't get yourself all worked up, Alice.

ALICE

Well, where is he? (*Suddenly anxious*) Maybe he's sick somewhere—or having a breakdown. Maybe I ought to notify the police.

CHRIS

Now don't worry about Bud. He can take care of himself.

ALICE

(*Grimly*)

Oh, he *can*, huh? I'm so glad to hear it.

CHRIS

I know Bud better than anybody. He'll come home again—and when he does you've got to be awfully smart and patient . . .

ALICE

(*Flatly*)

I do? Why?

(*The doorbell rings. She looks at it hopefully, then goes to it and opens it.* MRS. GANS *is revealed, looking very miserable. She carries a small overnight bag.*)

MRS. GANS

(*Lips trembling*)

Alice . . .

ALICE

Oh, hello, Mother. . . . What's the matter? (*She looks at bag*) Where are you going?

MRS. GANS

Oh, Alice . . . !

CHRIS

Hello, Mrs. Gans.

(MRS. GANS *looks at* CHRIS, *and tries to nod.*)

MRS. GANS

Hello, Chris . . .

(*She starts to sob, and sits.* ALICE *and* CHRIS *stare at one another bewilderedly.*)

ALICE

Mother—(*The phone rings. She turns, confused, then goes to it eagerly*) Hello? (*Her voice drops disappointedly*) Yes, he's here . . . (*Holds receiver to* CHRIS) It's your office, Chris . . . (*She goes to her mother, as* CHRIS *goes to the phone*) Mother, what *is* it?

(MRS. GANS *shakes her head.*)

CHRIS

(*Into phone*)

Yes? . . . Uh huh . . . Yes, I see. Okay . . . (*He hangs up*) Alice, I've got to run. I'll be back later. (*Takes* ALICE's *hands, smiles encouragement, and goes out*) Good-bye, Mrs. Gans.

ALICE

(*Turns to her mother*)

Mother, pull yourself together. What's the matter?

MRS. GANS

For thirty-five years I've kept my mouth shut—controlled my temper—put up with everything . . .

ALICE

What are you talking about?

MRS. GANS

For thirty-five years I've submerged my personality in his . . .

ALICE

Pop?

MRS. GANS

(*Scathingly*)

Yes—*Pop!* Well, I'm finished! I'm finished! I can't stand it any more! He can't talk to me like that! Mrs. Edgar Guest, huh? Well, I'm tired of being married to Arthur Godfrey!

ALICE

Oh, really! You're acting like a couple of two-year-olds!

MRS. GANS

(*Furiously*)

Oh, we are, huh? Just because it's *us! Our* problems are nothing, I suppose? You have *real* troubles!

ALICE

I'm sorry, Mother. Only you know Dad—he says a lot of things in the heat of the moment, but he doesn't mean them.

MRS. GANS

I'm tired of making allowances!

ALICE

When you're married, you've got to. . . . It's give and take . . .

MRS. GANS

(*Laughs scornfully*)

You're a fine one to talk!

ALICE

At least I *try*. . . .

MRS. GANS

Try . . . You don't know what trying is. . . . You've only had fifteen years, but I've had *thirty-five* of taking it, and I can't take it any more! He's blaming me for the whole thing—

ALICE

What whole thing?

MRS. GANS

What, she says! We're the laughingstock of all our friends! Since your daughter went on that program, we can't show our faces anywhere!

ALICE

Oh, I suppose *that's* my fault too?

MRS. GANS

No, your father says it's *my* fault. If I had been the right kind of mother, and chained you to the bedpost, sixteen years ago . . .

ALICE

That's a terrible thing to say!

MRS. GANS

I just hope your daughter doesn't follow your example.

ALICE

(*Sighs*)

I just hope she's held out *this* long.

MRS. GANS

Oh! I never should have come here in the first place! I'll go to a hotel!

ALICE

Now, wait a minute, Mother.

(*The doorbell rings. The door opens.* GANS *is revealed, looking miserable.*)

MR. GANS

(*Heavily*)

Hello, darling.

ALICE

Pop . . .

MR. GANS

(*Eyes* MRS. GANS)

Oh? Ran right over here? Couldn't wait, huh?

MRS. GANS

(*Sniffs*)

Huh! What are *you* doing here?

MR. GANS

(*To* ALICE)

Well, before you swallow everything, I'd like you to hear *my* side of the story.

MRS. GANS

I *told* her your side of the story.

ALICE

Pop, please! I don't want to hear *anybody's* side. I've got my *own* troubles.

(*She goes into kitchen.*)

MR. GANS

Now don't talk like that, darling. You and Bud have so much to be grateful for . . . (*Turns to* MRS. GANS, *wistfully*) Don't you think I'm right, Lillian?

MRS. GANS

(*Coldly*)

Don't ask *my* opinion. You've listened to Mrs. Edgar Guest for years. . . .

MR. GANS

Darling, I'm terribly sorry. I was excited, and I didn't realize what I was saying.

MRS. GANS

You never do.

MR. GANS

Darling . . . Darling . . . I'm terrible, I know, Lilly. (*Sits beside her for a moment trying to get an idea. Then sings*)

Lilly, Lilly of the valley
Come on, Lilly, let's get pally
Lilly, Lilly, you're the sweetest of the lot.
Be my Lilly-O
Be my Lilly-O
(*Kneels*)
And I'll be your flower pot.

MRS. GANS

(*Bursts into a laugh, and embraces him*)

Arthur, you're a nut. Half the fun of fighting with you is making up.

MR. GANS

Lilly, you know what we need?

MRS. GANS

What!

MR. GANS

A vacation! From daughters, son-in-laws, grandchildren, everyone. Lilly, I'm gonna take you on a trip.

ALICE

(*Enters from kitchen, sees* GANS *on knees*)
Pop! What are you doing?

MR. GANS

(*Jumps up hastily*)
Nothing, nothing. . . . Alice, I'm going to take Mother on a little trip.

(CHRIS *comes in.*)

CHRIS

Hello, folks . . . Alice . . .

ALICE

Yes?

CHRIS

That call I got from the office . . .

ALICE

Chris . . . There's nothing wrong?

CHRIS

No, nothing wrong. But I had a talk with Bud. He's fine.

ALICE

(*Coldly*)
Oh, he *is?* That's nice. Did he ask about us?

CHRIS

He's very upset, and very penitent . . .

MR. GANS

Of course he is!

CHRIS

He's miserable. He's been going through hell for the last four days. You can see it in his face.

ALICE

(*Icily*)

Haggard, is it?

CHRIS

Now, Alice. He wants to come home. He's so contrite—he'll do anything . . .

ALICE

There's nothing else he *can* do. He did it all before he left.

MRS. GANS

Darling, that's not fair.

MR. GANS

I feel sorry for the boy.

ALICE

Boy!

CHRIS

Open your heart, Alice. He wants to beg your forgiveness.

MRS. GANS

After all, Bud has been a good husband *most* of the time and . . .

ALICE

(*Breaks in sharply*)

What you *really* mean is, that you'd like to take a trip and you don't want to feel guilty about me or the kids, isn't that right?

MR. GANS

(*Guiltily*)

No—no . . .

ALICE

(*To* CHRIS)

And *you* want him because you're probably doing his work at the office with a bad back and you may lose Janice and her shampoo.

CHRIS

Now, how can you think such a thing?

ALICE

And the kids keep saying "Poor Pop." They want him back because he's a soft touch. But no one thinks about *me.* I'm not supposed to have feelings, or pride—just sit home and take it on the chin till he decides to come back.

CHRIS

(*Uneasily*)

Well, as a matter of fact, he *is* back. He's out in the hall right now, waiting for me to call him in.

(ALICE *stares in surprise.*)

ALICE

(Very grim)

Oh, he's waiting in the hall, is he? Now that's very moving. Gets you right here. (*She pats her heart mockingly*) Ask him in, Chris.

(CHRIS *goes to door.*)

MR. GANS

(Heartily)

That's my girl!

CHRIS

(Opens the door)

Bud, come on in! It's all fixed!

(BUD *comes in slowly, a sad little smile on his face, looking at* ALICE.)

BUD

(Softly)

Alice . . .

(OKKIE *and* DEBBIE *run in and throw themselves on him wildly.*)

DEBBIE

Pop, oh *Pop!*

OKKIE

Gee, Pop, you're home!

DEBBIE

It's been terrible around here.

BUD

Darling . . . Okkie . . .

OKKIE

You don't know how we missed you, Pop!

DEBBIE

Don't ever leave us alone again!

BUD

(*Staring at* ALICE)

I won't, kids, I promise.

CHRIS

Bud, this makes me very happy.

BUD

Thanks, Chris, I've been a damn fool.

CHRIS

Forget it. See you at the office Monday . . . (*Turns to* MR. *and* MRS. GANS) Amazing! Those doctors are right. It's psychosomatic. (*Indicates his back*) I don't feel a thing.

(*He does a dance step and goes, laughing.*)

MRS. GANS

Come on, Arthur, let's leave the children alone. Alice dear, just keep the cave clean . . . Wait till they come home, and then console them. They're children, just nutty children.

MR. GANS

Bud, it's been true since the dawn of time, go out with your spear . . . Kill a bear . . .

MRS. GANS

Now is the time, Arthur. (*She turns him and takes him out the door*) Good-bye all.

MR. GANS

Good-bye.

(*They go.*)

BUD

Kids, I'd like to talk to your mother alone. Would you leave us alone for a moment?

OKKIE

Oh, sure, Pop.

(*He grabs* DEBBIE *and pulls her off.* BUD *looks pathetically at* ALICE.)

BUD

(*Softly*)

Alice . . .

ALICE

(*Coldly*)

What, Bud?

BUD

Darling . . . I'm sorry . . .

(*He goes to her to take her in his arms. She sits down sharply. He stands looking foolishly down at her.*)

ALICE

You're sorry . . . Oh, well, as long as you're sorry, let's forget it. Is that it?

BUD

Now, Baby . . .

ALICE

Don't bother, Bud. Everybody's happy that you're back—but *me.*

BUD

You're right. What can I do to square it, Alice?

ALICE

I'm afraid a fast pitch isn't the answer. (*She rises, then quite calmly*) You see, Bud, I'm not as quick as the family to forgive and forget. Probably my mean side.

BUD

I know you better than that. You *have* no mean side.

(*He starts to take her in his arms, she ducks him deftly and smiles.*

ALICE

And don't give me that Fernando Arms approach, because that's not going to get you anywhere.

BUD

(*Reproachfully*)

Now, Alice . . .

ALICE

(*Crisply*)

You have an idea you can just walk out on me when you feel like it, walk back when you feel like it, open your arms and I'll fall right into them.

BUD

I didn't *have* any ideas. I was impulsive that's all, and I'm sorry.

ALICE

Well, I'm *not* impulsive. I'm doing this in cold blood. I'm leaving you, Bud.

BUD

Leaving? You can't do that.

ALICE

Why not? You did. Now it's my turn. Suppose you take care of the house and the children for awhile?

BUD

(Yells)

What the hell has got into you?

ALICE

You're still shouting, I see?

BUD

(Controlling himself)

Okay, quietly, we'll discuss it quietly. . . . *(Snaps again)* Only for the love of God will you drop that phony smile!

(MILLIE *comes in from kitchen.*)

MILLIE

Welcome back, Mr. W. I thought I heard you!

BUD

Hullo, Millie . . .

ALICE

Millie, I'll be going away for awhile. Ask Joe to bring my trunk and valises up from the basement.

MILLIE

Going away? Where you goin', Mrs. W.?

ALICE

I don't know yet, but I'll send my forwarding address. You'll have to take care of Mr. Walters and the children when I'm gone. I'm sure you can manage all right.

MILLIE

Yes, Ma'am.

(*She goes off, looking at* BUD *dubiously.*)

BUD

Washington's farewell to his troops. (ALICE *starts away. He takes her arm*) Oh, come on, Baby, we were going to discuss everything quietly.

ALICE

(*Laughs*)

I don't know what we have to discuss. You gave me the idea. When the strain and stress of marriage gets too much to bear, just go away till you get over it.

BUD

And how long do you think *that's* gonna take?

ALICE

In my mood, at least indefinitely.

BUD

Where are you going?

ALICE

I don't know. Maybe Mexico City. I hear it's cheap and colorful. I'm not sure. But it'll be out of the country.

(ALICE *exits. The phone rings.* BUD *stares after her, then answers it.*)

BUD

Hello? . . . Yes, just a minute . . . (*Calls off*) Alice! It's for you.

(ALICE *comes back into the room and goes to phone.*)

ALICE

Hello? . . . Oh, hello, Doctor . . . (*She listens*) Oh? I see . . . Died? . . . Oh, yes . . . Yes . . . I will . . . Thank you . . .

(*She hangs up with a grim, frustrated expression.*)

BUD

Who is it? Who died?

ALICE

Oh, my God . . . It's terrible . . . At a time like this . . .

BUD

(*Anxiously*)

Alice, what is it? Who died?

ALICE

Oh, let me alone! Don't touch me!

BUD

(*Frantically*)

But tell me—who was it—who died?

ALICE

The rabbit.

BUD

Rabbit? *What* rabbit?

ALICE

My test. I took a rabbit test.

BUD

(*Bewildered*)

A what?

ALICE

Oh, you fool! This could only happen to *me!* What good is it being a woman? We're trapped from the moment we're born!

BUD

You mean we're going to have a baby?

ALICE

Not *we—I'm* going to have a baby!

BUD

(*Dazed*)

Are you *sure?*

ALICE

Do you want to go to the rabbit's funeral?

BUD

Oh, darling, that's wonderful!

(*He tries to kiss her. She pushes him away.*)

ALICE

You keep away from me!

BUD

Alice—angel . . .

(*The doorbell rings.* BUD *goes to door and opens up. The same two delivery men stand there with another TV set.*)

FIRST MAN

(*Indicates* BUD *in awe*)

That's the party, all right.

SECOND MAN

It's kind of eerie, ain't it?

BUD

Come in . . . Come in.

(*He motions them to bring it in.*)

ALICE

(*Angrily*)

What *is* this? I never want to see another set again! What idiot, what fool, sent this one?

(*The men put it down quickly and hasten to door.*)

FIRST MAN

(*To* BUD)

Enjoy yourself, Jack—what the hell?

(*They laugh and go.*)

BUD

There's a card . . . (*He tears it off, and reads*) "Oh, my darling, this heart, so full of regret and tenderness, can not last without you . . . Our love is bigger than television, bigger than 'Howdy Doody,' bigger than 'Dragnet'—Forgive me" . . . (*He looks up at her*) It's signed, Bud . . .

ALICE

Oh, Bud, what can I do with you?

BUD

Take me, whatever I am, take me . . . (*He takes her in his arms*) What did you say your name was?

ALICE

Gans . . . Alice Gans . . .

(*They dance slowly.*)

BUD

My sweet little Alice Blue Gans . . .

ALICE

Oh, Mr. Walters, you're just terrible . . .

BUD

I know . . . Just terrible.

(MILLIE *enters from kitchen.*)

MILLIE

I couldn't help hearing the news, Mrs. W. Congratulations.

(OKKIE *and* DEBBIE *enter.*)

BUD

Thanks, Millie.

MILLIE

But I think it's only fair to tell you—I'll stay till the baby comes. But I ain't carrying any trays to no baby nurses.

ALICE

Really!

BUD

Thanks for the advance notice, Millie. We appreciate it.

OKKIE

Gee, what am I gonna tell the fellas at school? You havin' a baby at *your* age.

DEBBIE

And don't think you're gonna make a baby-sitter out of *me!*

BUD

(Yells)

ALL RIGHT!

(KIDS *and* MILLIE *rush off. The doorbell rings.* BUD *opens it and* HANDYMAN *enters with bedroom door.*)

HANDYMAN

Here's your bedroom door. The lock's all fixed now. Can I put it up?

BUD

(*Looks at* ALICE)

Sure. Go right ahead.

(HANDYMAN *carries it toward bedroom and goes out.*)

ALICE

(*Looks after* HANDYMAN, *then turns to* BUD)

That's fine. After the horse is stolen, they lock the stable door. . . .

(*They embrace as:*)

The curtain falls